It was Written

Kevin Wright

Editor Trish Knudsen, Illustration Ismat Rahman

iUniverse, Inc.
New York   Bloomington

It was Written

iUniverse books may be ordered through booksellers or by contacting:

iUniverse
1663 Liberty Drive
Bloomington, IN 47403
www.iuniverse.com
1-800-Authors (1-800-288-4677)

Because of the dynamic nature of the Internet, any Web addresses or links contained in this book may have changed since publication and may no longer be valid. The views expressed in this work are solely those of the author and do not necessarily reflect the views of the publisher, and the publisher hereby disclaims any responsibility for them.

ISBN: 978-1-4401-3846-1 (pbk)
ISBN: 978-1-4401-3847-8 (ebk)

Printed in the United States of America

iUniverse rev. date: 4/8/2009

Acknowledgements

First and foremost, this wouldn't be possible without Trish Knudsen; thank you with every inch of me. Ismat, what can I say about you, we went from the chicken store to doing this; it goes to show everything happens for a reason. Thank you for being such a big part of this. I first came with the intention in mind to re-create what I consider a classic, for the simple reason that I felt it needed to be done. This book is for Analise; we miss you, momma loves you child, and you're living in our memories. Your brother Kieran is going to grow up and do you proud. Momma and Pops hold you forever in their hearts like you wouldn't believe. Anne -thank you for just being that inspiration, and Larry thank you for just being a wonderful soul. God bless my nephews and Momma I love you. To my family, I love you guys. Sasha - thank you for just being a wonderful friend, and a great mom to my Goddaughter. Carolina, I simply love you. Bisi and T.T. my sisters from another, thank you for just being yourselves, true friends to the end. Leandra thanks for being a part of my life, I love you. Krystina you know what it is to the end. Pritha, if words could only express my joy for having you in my life. Marco and Hayden, what can I say about you. My brothers, you mean the world and more to me thank you. You two guys are an inspiration every day I wake up. Hayden you are brilliant and my brother, so thank you for just being a wonderful soul. Marco, you're something that I was hoping would come along in my life and that's being a friend, so thank you for being you. Sameena, thank you for your love and support, I truly love you. Vanessa - thank you for being the wonderful person that you are. Theresa, your words of wisdom have always been food for thought; thank you for the love and support. Tonya Kent, thank you for being my sister from the very start. I love you beyond what words can explain and you know that it will never change. To my mother, you are everything and more and I thank you for just being so nurturing and loving to your baby boy. Zee, my brother from another, thank you for instilling in me your knowledge and support. God bless you and your family. To Miss Carter, I love you more than words can explain; thank you for teaching me and being that inspiration.

I felt the need to come back and do it for so many reasons. My brother was shot, and that took so much out of me. It made me want to pick up the pen and pad and go for another go around. Truth be told, I couldn't do it, so I said to myself I'm going to go back to my roots, to where it all started, and re-create something. This is for him, and he knows it's love and forever will be love. He's changing me in the smallest ways, and creating a new being in me which I have to thank him for. I have a rejuvenated sense of life because of his words and encouragement. Rosa, this seems like the beginning of something special, and I will walk you into the light sweetheart. I have lost a lot of people over the past couple of years; they're in a better place now, and we shall all meet again. I hope this book is more than just a book of words; something to think about. I hope to spark thoughts and influence minds. We shall overcome every obstacle put in front of us. The next day shall be brighter in every sense, shape and form. My words will live beyond my time and this is what I was set out to do. With that said, smile and enjoy my life, fun, laughter and tears. I put my heart into this so take it for what it's worth; simply something to look forward to. Love live life.

THEY PAINT THE MANY PICTURES
THE LITTLE FISH IN A BIG POND
THEY DEPICT ME TO BE
FIGURING I'M THROUGH WITH IT,
I'VE GOT THE MIND OF A HUSTLER
HEART OF A KING
I'VE SEEN MYSELF THROUGH
THE ENDLESS STRUGGLE
HOPING FOR BRIGHTER DAYS
FAILING TO PAY ME MY RESPECT
GARNERED
I CONTINUE TO WALK THE STREETS
SEARCHING FOR THE UNKNOWN
FIGHTING TO LIVE
DYING TO GIVE
MISERY SEEMS TO BE MY STATE OF
MIND
I REMAIN DESTINED TO FIND
A PEACE OF MIND
THIS HEART OF MINE
THROUGH HELL, FIRE, AND BRIMSTONE
GLADLY RISKING IT ALL

LETTER TO JUNGLE CITY

Verbal graffiti, throw the paint against the wall; let it create something unheard of. Let the thoughts be heard, let me speak to the few that will listen. I have an open ear to the city and the shots that ring off and the many that were left for dead. I miss my brothers, and I would do anything to bring you back even though some of you left havoc on the streets. The mothers have struggled, and all they have done is recycle the useless fathers and that goes out to the many of you who have failed to take care of our future kings and queens. I can't respect a lot of the men I see because they left their kids to play in the streets, and that shit burns a hole in my heart. This is not a subliminal shot at any man or woman; but to tell you truth, for the people that know me know I could care less who I offend for that matter. I sparked a thought in your minds, and you feel as though it's a shot at you. It helps me sleep at night, because you know that you're a useless soul.

I miss my city and everything that came with it; from Circle B, to the bridge, to the other side. To my people on the corners guzzling a 40, I feel your struggle. We're not oppressed and we shall overcome; that's to the death of me, till there is nothing left of me. I love subliminal shots and the beef that comes with it. We have no idea what beef is, it's not like we were in the sandbox yesterday. We used to meet and settle our differences the real way. It's become a lost art and unheard of anymore. All of sudden we forgot to put our fists up and do it like we used to. When you listen to me and read on, let it sink in, what I'm truly trying to say. Let the words flow, and forget about what you're trying to hear, rather let it be heard. When you decide to go out and commit a crime with another person, realize that it was your decision. You live by the gun and you will die by the gun; that's your faith whether you make that choice or not. I wish some of you would go back to the sandbox and fight because we got tough behind our guns, because they bust. I don't respect the shooter; especially if he shoots like a bitch. I would love to meet all of you in the school yard again because shit would definitely have a different turn out, and that's word to God.

I grew up in the era watching the pizza man get robbed and that was reality. This is my city and I wouldn't take any of it back. I learned how to fight, break faces, and most importantly, I learned the meaning of loyalty. Loyalty is dead because I have my brother shooting my brothers. I haven't heard anyone say my name in all of this and it's good, but it's bad because they must have forgotten how I get down. Not brave enough to let the gun bust, but I'll stomp the next man who steps to my throne. Ask the rat who gave a statement; I don't respect written statements that's Omar's job to make. Street credibility has gone down the drain and I don't respect a lot of dudes walking with their heads up. Lucky is lucky; he left the bus with a few scratches; last I heard he ran from that fight. More or less we saved his life when the dude, who shall remain nameless, stomped his face out and I came to his rescue. Some of you are lucky you have a mouth to speak with, being in my presence. This is not tough talk, these are a few words from the horse's mouth, and I just said it. I think what people fail to realize is that reality is what it is; if we didn't have freedom of speech or a platform from which to speak, , where would we be today? A lot of things wouldn't exist. Rosa Parks sat on that bus and Martin gave that sizzling speech that remains etched in my heart.

I fail to recognize the history because all I can remember is a system that's been corrupted, and failed to teach me about my leaders; the office that is full of democratic bullshit. Some of you are beating rape charges and murder charges, and I have to sit down and think about where it is I live. My words feel jailed, like the people who fail to see daylight. Truth be told, I've been sitting back just taking the backseat, watching the bullshit that's been taking place. They must have forgotten how I get down. Lack of evidence and witnesses, who is to blame? Not everyone can be a snitch like Spilla, or be a bitch like Lucky; fuck a street name and fuck your street credibility. I took that shit and flushed it down the toilet along with the other shit you been saying. They call me Lefty, and that's for the simple fact that I've been cracking you motherfuckers in the jaw since you were born and you've never won a fight. Ask my momma; ask your momma, you've never won a fist fight.

You worship the motherfucker who ran the streets with his head cut off. He forgot where he came from and forgot the people that put him on. In essence I feel like he lost his soul in so many ways, and don't get it misconstrued, I still miss big homie. No matter what, they can never take back the time he and I spent together. I wish I could take away the guns, and create more laughter, but on the flip side of things I have to create something in order for people to listen. I feel like my words have fallen on deaf ears and I'm more than what you can imagine. When I said I'm back on the block, what I meant by that was I took a stroll through and I didn't see anyone; I heard the wind and the lost souls who whispered to me. They wish they could be different when they had the chance to be. Fatherless children and single parents' homes haunt me because I want to be there for them but I cannot. All I can offer is a few words to the people that will listen. I fail to be like the rest of them because I'm not them, and I could never be them. There are so many of them I don't respect, they were my brothers and now we stand on the lines of not speaking. That's not to say I have an issue with them, and I want to go that route, but trust me if they want to fight you know I've always been down and I will always be down, just name the time and place. Put your gun down was just a warning shot for the few who would listen; don't forget where you came from, or the people that created the platform that allowed you to even be able to speak. I tried to create an understanding where we could all grow together and take it to another level; where we could all be financially stable and create a new space. You fail to hold that dream that I once held, from learning how to read and failing at everything you do to this very day. Fatherhood is not a fucking joke, so when your kid runs out on you just chase them and hold them tight and the tell them that you love them.

The mothers are missing sons and the daughters have become pregnant, it feels like the ghetto has been mental telepathy. Babies are having babies before the age of 15. They were running around slack as the wristlets selling their soul for attention or comfort. I miss home and everything that came with it. The crew was like the family, and the battlefield was just epic, we respected it and that's what would stand for. In America they fight for the red, white, and blue; over here it's survival and who's gun can bust. I hear the guns bust and no fists fly. Dwayne Taylor, brother I miss you, it hurt a lot when I heard you died. I told you come see me so we could reminisce on old times of me crossing you over and the funny games of horse we played in the gym. Life isn't fair but we have to make the best of it. That's why when God deals us our cards we have to save the aces. I have a few up my sleeve, homie. "Pieces to a Dream" and "Far from Home" are incredible bodies of work. As I try to recreate a classic in my eyes, I can't help but remember the good old times and the people I have had the pleasure to meet such as you homie. I see Ricky from time to time and I give him a hug and show him the love we all had. I haven't seen Dog, but I'm sure you're up there watching me write this piece and thinking to yourself, he is that kid. I hope your kids grow up to be something special and do everything they can ever dream of; brothers.

I don't miss the snitches and the people that forgot to make phone calls. I love my people, JBO Ice, Jason Knight, Meth, K-9, Hustlemann, to name a few. It's love when I see you, and to the rest walk your path and I shall walk mine. I love my city and the people that created the history behind it; without them I wouldn't be who I am today. I feel like I struck a nerve in a few people in a few lines, subliminal shots hurt the most; the issues that follow it and the result at the end of the day. At the end of the day I don't need anyone to help me out; no co-sign, the war is with me and comes from within. It's what I have to battle with each and every day of my life. I battle with the past and the things I couldn't control. The present, however, has me consumed with what I could possibly do to make it better. My words will slowly be heard, and I will take that along with the memories I have. My soul will live past so many people and that's a fact, not a promise. I left my mark and I've done all I have needed to do, so when my time comes so be it. I wish I could say more names but at some point I have to realize being politically correct is an option, as ignorant of a person I am. This is chess not checkers; these are warning shots, if I see moves being made I'll give you what I got. ..

To be continued........

DREAMS

Momma told me, "The lights are out son, the bill needs to be paid; the only thing free in this world is government water." Lost in the darkness as it placates my memories; walking through that dark house, up the steps, to my room where only the darkness can console my tears. Under my bed was that money I saved for nothing that was something; still trying to make sense of life and what it was. Money I didn't know, the only thing that appeared was its texture and that almighty number that kept me consistent. I knew not the words to describe it; it was of no importance to me because I had already given away so much for some worthy cause.

So many days, so many memories, as I try to recapture the images, the many pictures; no dreams, full of dreams, I'm not sure. Sense of reality has always been a difficult thing for me as a result of expectation. Expectation has always exceeded everything that existed in life, as I painted life as it was supposed to be or wanted it to be. Reality was always so hard to accept, asking myself if this was actually life. If this was life, I don't want to live anymore; head dumped underwater for these almighty sins, as he defined it. I ask myself every day what the fuck do they know about rape? Whether this fucking system is full of fuckery? Or is my language valid as content for the people who read it? Am I actually free? Do they even care? Am I what I appear to be? What is it they see? The words and the way I carry myself, is it of importance? Should I grab a gun and blow his fucking head off? Truth be told, when I catch the kid on my own I'm going to put him in a body bag; before he dies I'll ask him if it was worth it. Stolen identity, foolish pride, motherfuckers need to reside. Is this really me who speaks of this violence? Or my inner soul? Is it pain that corrupts my inner thoughts? Pressure busts pipes, lights get wiped away, two solid fucking paragraphs to let you know what I'm really about. The streets will never define my character, but my words will. Temperatures rise, the sun goes down, to appear at early morning as I awake to a new day reflecting on life itself. Life is not what it is; it's what you make it. If I had a clip I would leave off few rounds in your fucking skull, shit it's traumatizing like you could never imagine. She's still fucked but I guess God is the creator and we shall leave it up to him to decide your faith. If I walk by you and I have nothing to say, it's because I'm not ok!

I don't want to close my eyes
I don't want to fall asleep
Cause I'll miss you baby
I don't want to see you go

Afraid if I sleep
Wake up
You'll be gone forever
That will tear me apart

For the days I saw you
Always a bright day
Always made my day
When I was down
You brought me to life
For that I thank you

I don't know you
Yet I feel like I do
I dream of you
Yet it can't be true

I want you to feel my love
Yet I don't know if you want to feel
I want to share my feelings
Yet you have none

As I sit here
Steering at you
Thinking of what it would be like
To have you as mine
Everything I want
Everything I need
Why can't we succeed?

You're like a star
A star that's hard to reach
I try so hard
So hard to reach that star
Though I cannot reach it
I go through endless amounts
Endless amounts of trying

I sit at night
At night staring at that star
Wondering when and if
When and if I'll ever reach that star
My heart says try
I say give up
The only way out
To follow
Follow my heart
Maybe someday
Someday I'll reach that star
Until then
I'll keep on trying

My first love
The first time I found it
I lost it
I tried to hold on to it
But couldn't

I felt you were the one
You're everything
Everything to dream of
Everything to wish for
Everything to capture

You brought me joy
I feel such pain
Such pain of losing you
You never have anything
Till you lose it
Everything I dreamed of
Is now gone

AFTER MY DEPARTURE

LET ME REST AND BE WEARY

DO NOT SHED A TEAR

FOR I AM NOT OUT IN THE COLD

NOR AM I LEFT ASTRAY

I STAND BESIDE OUR LORD SAVIOUR

JESUS CHRIST

I AM WITH HIS SON

FAR NOT FROM YOU

SO CLOSE WITHIN YOUR HEART

MY SOUL RESTS

MY SPIRIT FOREVER LIVES ON

LET ME DIE AT PEACE TO MIND

Tell me girl
Who's going to love you?
For the person you are?
Things you do?

Tell me girl
Who's going to be your friend?
As well as your man?
Who's going to be there?

Tell me girl
Who's going to hold you like I do?
Kiss you like I do?
Make love to you like I do?
Spend the way I do?
Most important
Love you like I do?
Nobody girl

You're there as a friend
As well as a lover
Most important
You're for us

When I was down
You brought me to my feet
You were there
That extra ear
You blended advice and opinion
You gave me time
Lots of laughs
Thank you

You came before me
I was last
Few minutes set us apart
Inseparable we were
Always at sides

Our parents
Described us, a sensation
To this generation
Special deep within their hearts

We grew
Only but closer
Felt each other's pain
Down together

Feeling each other's pain
Thinking each other's thoughts
Knowing each other's minds
What's so special?
We both are

I walk everyday
Confused in every way
Confused about you
The things you do

Whenever I was there
You didn't treat me fair
Thinking about what you mean to me
I wish you could see

When does this end?
It all depends
Which way we go
That I don't know
Is it over?

Where my heart is?
Indeed my heart is with you
My sun in the morning
Moon at night
What I wake up for
Sleep on
Dream of every night
I long for every moment
To be with you
Hold you
In my arms
I feel not at my inside
Your point of view
These are just some of the ways
I feel about you

Oh girl
You broke my heart
I gave you the world
Let you come live with me
I gave you the world

I remember those times
Walking the hills
Through the fields
Pick you a flower
Give you a sweet kiss
Tell you I love you
I remember those times
As if it were yesterday
So memorable

Oh girl you broke my heart
It was fun while it lasted
But it's over

All I feel
Is pain and sorrow
It's like no one
No one cares
Cares what I feel
Cares what I think
I feel like a rock
Rock at the bottom
Bottom of the ocean
There but nobody cares
People speak
It is as if
I were invisible
I feel so alone
I feel like no one cares
About me
I wish it all
All would change

What I dream about is you
Yet it can't be true
Dreaming of seeing you
Holding you
Kissing you

As I feel this kiss tonight
Feels so meant to be, so right
You in my sight
Shining so bright
Though it's just a dream
If only it could be reality

Wished for you
On a shooting star
Wondering where you are
Here you've come
Now I want you to go
Why is that so
Cause I can't achieve
If you'd believe
In me I am everything
Can't you see?
I'm for you
You for me
I cross your mind
Not hard to find
Right here
Waiting for you
To walk in my life experience love
So believe
We were meant to be

Brand new is the glimmer in my eyes
Brand new is your smile
Every refreshing is the taste of your lips
Forever wanting is your comfort
The sea savors the salt as I do your love
Love is that quenching thirst
Thirst is forever more
More is you
Enough is not us
Us is the sky about and beyond
Beyond are my thoughts
Thoughts of a dream
Dream of everyday brand new
Brand new is my love
My love is you
You are my love
My love is everything and more
More, more, more
I pour kisses into a cup
Drink my love
My love

Love is waiting
Love is watching
Love is listening
As well do

Love is (to) succeed
So it is to fail
Tempting conscience
Bringing such happiness along its path
Sadness as well

Love is time
It is to reach
Capture and be held
Never to let go
Most importantly
Love is deep
Deeper than the sky itself
It is to be cherished
Never longing to die

Feelings shared
Hearts broken
Dreams shattered
Future seeming evident
Energy and sweat
Love not forget
Heart and soul
Things unfold
What is thought to be true
Doesn't stick like glue
What was prominent to heart
Turned out destiny with no start
What in your heart was prominent
Not close to dominant
Now in your heart
Is you, torn apart

My heart is broken
My soul you've taken
Taken half of me
For which you can't see
My love for you so deep
That you did sweep
Your love I cherished
For which that has perished
Your love I adored
That you ignored
Our life together similar to a feather
That blew away
Lurking never to stay
Taking its place
In holy grace
Never to return
Now adjourned

You question my feelings
You question my thoughts
You question my heart
You question my past
As well my experience
You question me
My every desire
To be with you

What I question
Your feelings for me
Your desire to be with me
When together
I've felt you drifted away
To another dimension
Some other world unknown
Yet I still love you
Since you've arrived
I've witnessed nothing but happiness
Repairing my broken heart
Giving me a piece of life to hold
And another reason for enjoying life

In such a short time
I fell in love
When with you
I feel the comfort and security
Knowing no alarm
Close to me someone that cares for me
Ask yourself
Am I right?

I will forever love
To the holy sky
And up above
My heart's been broken
My soul's been taken
Yet I still will forever love

I live to honour thy love
To live to share
Most importantly
I live to care

Love seems right
Love seems wrong
It will forever live on
Love is life
Life I love
It is and forever will be
As white as a dove

I promise to you
I'm a true man
So I vow to you
I'll be here for you
To love and to care
To hold and to share
I promise you
All my love
Not promising the stars
Promising my heart
So it is here I start
To offer all I have
Every inch of me
Here you will see
True love to your eyes
I promise you life
Full of love and happiness
I promise
The love you need
I promise
You mean the world to me
You come first
You're the only one
I want in my life

I can't get you off my mind
All these years
I've looked for that someone
That someone to make a difference in my life
I think you may be that special one

When I'm alone
I long for that day
The day for us to be together again
Never going a day without a thought of you to mind
Loving you gives warmth to my soul
All I can do
Is think about you
I love you
From the bottom of my heart

All day thinking
All day thinking about you
All the times we shared together
Countless moments
The love we had for one another
The memories won't be forgotten

Sometimes I feel so alone
Wondering what to do
To get you off my mind
I do everything
Coming to the realization that I can't
You're everything I need
Everything I want
Can't you be the one for me?
I never thought
Thought you would come along
Never thought I'd find love
Till the day I found you
Love is tough to let go
I know we have to let our feelings die
You'll always be in my heart

I miss you
Yet you haven't been gone to long
Feels like forever
To see you again

I woke up
First thing to my eyes
I saw your picture
Painted on the wall
More than a thousand words
Couldn't describe

You brought joy to my life
I want you
In my life

The only lie was he
    The only truth was me
        To good to be real
    Words he speaks are unworthy of his existence
            His mouth should be wired shut
                Mine Spewing words of wisdom
                Mind beyond wisdom itself
            Words I speak have been jailed for a minute
                I am here for nothing?
                Or am I here for something?
                    My words move sense
                    Sense moves cents
                    Cents create dollars
                    They say dollars
                        create dreams
                        I beg to differ
                            I'm walking with
                            this dream
                    Words from the Heart
                        I bring you
                    Pieces to a Dream

Sweet and tender
That is what you are
That is why I want to reach this star
Feeling that touch
That sense of warmth
Your body compressed to mine
While love blows in the air
As I stare into your eyes
I pop my surprise
I kiss you

At this point in time
You don't feel secure with me
Maybe I'm not right for you
Maybe I am
Your actions leave me confused
With nothing to do
I feel trapped
My heart feels alone
The path I follow
I stand at a dead end
Wondering where to go
That I don't know
At this point in time
Though I feel this way
I still want to stay
Within your arms with no alarm
Staring into the deep blue sky
I look and testify
That I love you

So how does it feel?
With my lips caressing your face
Your sexy sensuous body
All I need right now
Is you beside me
So you could see
While I'm writing this
Me blowing you a kiss
You on my mind
I fantasize overtime
Your love I cherish
For which shall never perish
My love for you
So true

An angel walked into my life
Who could be my wife
You've repaired this broken heart
From the very start
You are my destiny

I poured out my heart
I poured out my soul
I told you my hopes I told you my dreams
I told you my fears
Yet that wasn't enough

Your love was so sweet
You made my life complete
In return lies and deceit
Your love I did adore
That will perish forever more
All that I have
Is now forever gone
The one I called wife
Has now left my life
I wonder is it me?
Or there is a future that I do not see
A future full of love
I wish and I hope
For sunny days

She feels my love
Yet I feel not hers
She expresses her love
I fail not expressing mine
She speaks her mind
I speak words not of my own
She shows and expresses her feelings
I lack in attempt to mine

I can't change
She can't change
We both
Feel different about each other

It's tearing me up
To watch her leave my sight
Such pain and abrupt
Eating me up
Heart feels so weak

Trying to get over witnessing her go
Standing there watching, saying later
Forbidding the word
Goodbye uttering from my very depths

Never saying goodbye
Words coming from her
I love you
Then a hug
Watching her walk out my life

I sit here day and night
Night and day
Thinking about you
As if you were my sun, moon, stars
They are things
Things that cannot be reached

As I sit here
Wondering what
Wondering what it would take
Take to win your heart
Your heart is
Is a vital key
To a part
Part of my life
To win your heart
Would be similar
Similar to reaching
Reaching the sun, moon and stars

For your love
I'd run the extra mile
Climb the highest mountain
No matter how high

For your love
I'd swim the ocean
No matter how far
How steep

For your love
I'd do endless tasks
Just to achieve your love
I'd do anything

My love for you
Is endless
For your love
Is my love

That lost one
I lost her
She was special
I tried to hold on
Had to let go

One kiss
Had me shook
I was on her
Like white on rice

There was something special
I was trying to find
I succeeded
She was that one
The toughest thing
I had to let go

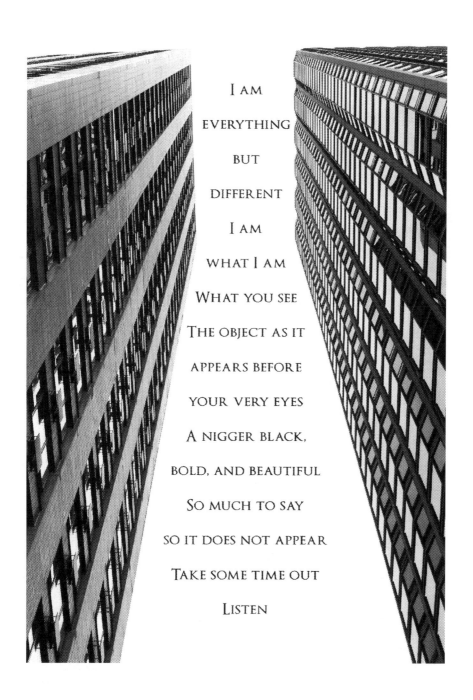

I AM

EVERYTHING

BUT

DIFFERENT

I AM

WHAT I AM

WHAT YOU SEE

THE OBJECT AS IT

APPEARS BEFORE

YOUR VERY EYES

A NIGGER BLACK,

BOLD, AND BEAUTIFUL

SO MUCH TO SAY

SO IT DOES NOT APPEAR

TAKE SOME TIME OUT

LISTEN

I feel such pain
Pain and abrupt
Since you broke
Broke my heart
My love for you
Higher than the sky itself

How could you
Destroy what we shared
What we had
We vowed
Vowed to stay together
Together for all eternity
Now look
Look what has become of us

It was the place
Where they mourned
Over his death
Standing there
Knowing it was the last time
They would witness his body's presence
Standing there
Recalling all memories
Rejuvenating the happiness once felt
Saying goodbye

My feelings for her
Were slowly dying
I tried so hard to find
But was unable
To capture that passion
I once fulfilled

For the time we shared
It was fun
Too bad
It has to end this way
I guess that's
Goodbye

I will remember you
The question that lurks,
Will you remember me?
I know I will
Memories of you are countless
My love for you so deep
Existing beyond the sky itself
As I sit here
Thinking how much I love you
Holding you and kissing your soft skin
Nothing I want to do more
Than for you to feel this love
Every night every day
In every way

As I sit at night
Staring to the stars
Wondering when
Romance may pass my direction
As I lay down
Thinking of that lucky star
Wondering when I can reach out
Hold on and capture it once again
Never to let go

It seems impossible
To reach the sky
Without the given tools needed
To capture that star
One day will arrive
Until then
I'll keep dreaming

If I may
If I might
Can I get with you tonight?
I want to caress your body
Kiss you in the right way
Touch you in the sweetest way
Run my fingers up your spine
Tell you you're mine

Tonight's the night
Don't put up a fight
Let's make this right
The stars are burning bright
You in sight
Can't you see?
This night was meant to be

Yesterday we met
Today we fell in love
Tomorrow we break up
(To be continued)

10. Thou shall live to love
9. Thou shall know love is the key to life
8. Thou shall never forget love
7. Thou shall know love is deeper than the sky itself
6. Thou shall express thy love
5. Thou shall conquer love
4. Thou shall cherish thy love
3. Thou shall love and honour thy mate
2. Thou shall not break ones heart
1. Thou shall love onto thee

He is a sensation
That sparks a generation
A big part of life
Touching you
From becoming a boy
To becoming man

Teaching you about life
All the triumphs and challenges
To face
Growing up as a young man
Is not so easy
They're supposed to guide steps to that way
Never being alone

Such a need for him
That person to look up to
Seeing through thick and thin
Always at that side
Through those times of need
He understands
Most importantly
He is a father

I'M FROM THE STREETS
THE STREETS RAISED ME
I'VE BECOME IMMUNE TO IT
NEVER BEEN BAPTIZED
BELIEVED TO HAVE CAUGHT A SPIRIT AT LEAST THREE OR FOUR TIMES
PEOPLE CONTINUE THAT SAME RHYME
EVERY DAY AND EVERY WEEK

THIS IS I
THE IMAGE YOU SEE
GOD GIVEN MIXED WITH SO MUCH
DIRT ON MY HANDS
NOT AN ANGEL HEAVEN SENT
A BEING LIKE SO MANY THAT WALK
JUST ANOTHER INDIVIDUAL

AN INSPIRATION I AM
AN INSTRUMENT WITH A VOICE
HERE FOR A REASON
EXPLORING MY SOUL IN THIS GLOBE
IN SEARCH OF THAT VIBRATION
AN ABUNDANCE OF DEDICATION
A ROSE IN CONCRETE
A CARD IN A FULL HOUSE
ONE BEING
ONE VOICE
ONE MIND
LET ME BE HEARD

I feel so lonely
Wondering what
What to do
To ease this pain
Ease this pain that I feel

Sometimes it is as though
Nobody cares
Cares about me
Just feeling so alone
Nobody looks
Looks out for me
I am a lone soul
With nothing though it seems
As I look
Look at life itself
I wish
Wish it would all just change

Who am I?
What do you see?
Judge me
Yet you won't see
That true sense of me
Things that I've seen
Places that I've been
Many things I've experienced
The life I was subject to live
Look inside
I have nothing to hide
 Take what you see for your worth
Find the truth
Whatever it is you proclaim
Judge me

I needed someone to hold
Someone to love
Suddenly an angel fell from the clouds
I looked above watching it fall so gracefully
Asking myself do I deserve all this?
She replied with a sweet kiss
Love beckoned upon me that moment
It was mine to own
Mine to begin with
Known from there as my dear
Inseparable from the start
She gained a place in my heart
Our love etched in stone never to be forlorn

A killer smile
To make you senile
Beauty as pure as gold
Someone to hold
Everything to want
Everything to dream
Rich as cream
Personality to die for
A wish to love forever more
One in life to call my wife
Someone to mention
Grabbing all attention
As a matter a fact she's all that

What is life?
Life is like a big obstacle
In front of you
When it slows you down
Just when you're there
You're back at a start

Life
It has its ups and downs
Highs and lows
But that just the way it goes
It's full of a lot of things
More important
You live it everyday
Your life

Yesterday we met
Today we fell in love
Tomorrow we'll break up
Yesterday words were said
Today kisses were felt
Tomorrow a heart will be broken
Yesterday was full of so much happiness
Today love was felt
Tomorrow-shed tears
Yesterday we talked on the phone
Today we were home
Tomorrow - separate

I feel the pain
You inflict upon yourself
Out of self-pity
So much pain agony and suffocation
The problems you can't bear to handle
Those which I want to dismantle

So close to me
That you cannot envision
Such a bond
That I think is so fond
I want you in my life
But you cause me such strife

Thoughts of you night and day
For that every day
I pray wishing for you home
So we can create this dome
A dome where such a family can grow again
Building such a dynasty
When this day reaches its existence
I will be relieved of my pain

As I sit here
Writing this masterpiece
In hopes of causing a catastrophe
Corrupting within your heart
In a good way
In hopes you will stay

How I feel
In such words I will reveal
Relieving you not off my mind
For you are so divine
Such thoughts on my mind night and day
Such thoughts flow every step of the way
Thoughts of you driving me crazy
Pictures of you within my arms
Such a person
Such a human being
You're all I want
Craving for you
So I end it there
Hoping without the result of tears
Then the scare
Of me getting over you

You said you hated me
You said you loved me
Is this really you?
Or what you say really true?
Am I this person?
Full of such hatred
Full of such cruel intentions
Is this really me?

When you place your eyes upon me
What is it you see?
Is it happiness or fulfillment?
Tears of joy?
Is it I who bears a heart?
Such soul for that matter?
Who am I?
What is it that is true?
What is it that is wrong?
What is it you hold on to holding back?
What is it you conceal?
Need it be revealed?
The truth

DARKNESS PLACATES THE CITY FULL OF SUCH BRIGHT LIGHT
RED STOP SIGNS AND YELLOW LINES
LOVE FILLS THE AIR
SUCH PLACES TO GO
SUCH A PERSON TO SEEK
BEHIND SOME DOOR
HIDDEN AMONGST THE SHADOWS
OPEN SUCH A MIND NOT OBLIVIOUS TO LOVE
SUCH A PAIN CANNOT BE FELT
TEARS THAT BLEED
FLOODING THE VERY STREETS
YOU CANNOT FEEL THIS LOVE AMONGST THE CLOUDS
DEEPER THAN THE VERY SKY ITSELF
PAIN NO MORE
LOVE SEEKS SUCH A SHALLOW TO FIND
IN THE MIST OF THIS VERY LIFE

Since the day
You took those baby steps into my life
Placing your eyes upon me
Spoken words
Fooling with my love and emotions
Since I've had vivid pictures
Brought to my surface
Visioning S+K=Love
Such an equation
Became my reality

Choosing you to experience love at hand
Feeling that comfort
Sharing what we have
To bond
Adding to such a prosperous life as it seems
Feelings of safeness and security
Have I found it?
Time will tell
Have I found love?
Or do I face disappointment
It holds in our hands

She's crazy about me
I wish you could see
My love, she fails to overcome
My heart she broke
Ripped and shredded to pieces

Now I embark on a new destiny
Something new to be reborn
Your feelings for me so strong
For we do belong
You've fooled with my love and emotions
Granted I have this potion
In hopes of you to drink
What I wish for

Her feelings for me bother you
What you need to be is true
Think of me and me only
What it's about
Is you and I
Nothing standing in our path
Walk with me face this task
Making love work for change

I stand no placement in your heart
What I thought I had
I feel no more for it
Not knowing where I stand
What I feel to heart
Us drifting apart
Tell me it isn't so?
I feel to not let go

As I see you pass by
I utter a hi
Asking myself
Do I deserve all this?
All I ask is one kiss
You show no devotion
In means to my emotion
I'm trapped is it just me?
Is this you?
You tell me

I steer into the deep blue sunset
Asking myself why
Is it you causing me all this pain
Why is it you cause me to suffer?
Why is it I deserve all this
Where did I go wrong?
All I've given is love
Love like never before
Care for your special love
Caring for your love forever more
I've poured out all I have
Until every ounce I have no more
Anything you've wanted and fathom to dream
I gave
Nothing I have saved
Nothing I hold back
Nothing I've lacked
My heart's for you in you and all you
Forever more
If all this is a crime
Convict me guilty where I stand

You played with my heart
You played with my soul
All I needed was someone to hold
You've walked in my life
You've walked out of my life
All you've done is cause me strife
You've left me down
Causing me to frown

It scares me to think of you
Wondering if you were true
As I sit here
Wondering where
In all this I stand
All I wanted was to be your man
Is this true?
Or am I left sad and blue
Till this day
I remain confused
I feel used
All these games
Yet you still come around
Fool with my emotions
All the games need to stop
Cause I cannot bear anymore

There's a reason I can't seem to get you off my mind - I don't want to. My deep inner self holds deep inner emotions, a strong passionate love that yearns for you.

Full of such courage
Full of such love
Amazing willpower
Brilliant in everyway
Role model to all
Never to fall
Her words of advice
Seem always so nice
Mother of all
So much to say
So much to share
So much to care
Heart so pure
Soul so deep
Nothing but goodness
She is unique

Inside I hold a lot of fears
Fears for which I shed tears
Fears, which I hide
Always remaining in denial
Waiting for an open fresh breath of air
The right time to utter
Though I continue this rhythm
Contemplating the same issues
I keep this concealed
Waiting to be revealed

I'd give anything
To touch your succulent lips
I want to feel that sweet kiss
Nothing I want to miss
This opportunity at hand
Dying to be that lucky man
Holding your hand
Body compressed to mine
The taste of sweet wine
As we intertwine
To share what is meant to be

THE WORLD IS ONE
A NATION
A COUNTRY
THIS PLANET EARTH
THAT CAN'T CORRESPOND
POVERTY IT IS
A DOLLAR THE CASE
THE STREETS IS WAR
PEOPLE HATE AND DECEIVE
THIS LIFELESS WORLD
MOTIONING FOR PEACE
BREATHES OF LOVE
LIFE'S A GIFT
CHERISH IT

Live alone
Die alone
Independent is who I am
Alone is where I stand
Friends, I have none
Trust is not my belief system
Love I have very little
This life I live everyday
Understand me
Believe in me
Know me
Not an option
I am
Who I am
My beliefs
I believe in

You have your view
You make your perception
You have opinion
You have truth to facts
Whether fact or opinion
View or perception
You have no clue
To what takes place
You judge me
From what you've grasped
You don't see me
You pain an image
I'm seen as that image
Not really who I am

A kiss
For a kiss
A hug for a hug
My heart
For your heart
My life
In your life
A lifetime
For all eternity
Together we share what is meant to be
A love everlasting

On a special day
I fell in love
Unlike no other
She pounded my heart
Touched my soul
Like no other
She touched me
Kissing me
Like no other
Held me
Never to let go
Like no other

It's been seven years
Since you've passed
Yet we still mourn
Still shedding those dotted tears
Never a day going by
Thoughts of you not crossing

There's a picture
Etched in my heart
Never to be torn apart
Brothers to the end
Though you put to sleep
Your soul laid to rest
You now have peace at mind
You're free
Free to watch over us
As we live our lives

As I watch you sit
Built up with emotions
Bottled up inside
Is an issue you wish to parish?

Tears and frustration
Cause your loss of concentration
Confused and cold
Looking for someone to hold
As I look within you
I can't imagine how you feel
You control you
As well your emotions
I see what you see
Could this all be?

No compassion
No heart
No love
Feels no way
Born to suffer
A life of pain
Full of negativity
With no end result
A troubled life
Full of corruption
Many tears most important
Hurt mentally

Never forced to triumph
But to fall down
Forced with no decision
To endure life at rock bottom

A life behind
New life waiting ahead
Many regrets
A lot to be proud of
Many times
Trials of suffocation
Though times of fame
Filled with glory
Left many to stand
A lot to look up
Stand happy and proud
While living on

No emotional distress
No tears
Shared feelings
Held within
Hurt mentally
Trapped
No comfort
Lost forever
Lies and deceit
To the bitter end and defeat
The truth withheld
Feelings of betrayal
Left alone
To live in this misery

One life to live
Letting not a day pass by
So many days dark and confused
Mentally and spiritually dead at times
More days have transgressed this rhyme

This is the life
High as ever, no hydro
So much to never ignore
Intoxicated by the struggle
So many trying times
As days go by they progress this rhyme

One life to live
This is the life
So much to claim
Living up to the name
As that pulse beats by

Warmth of a woman
Comfort of a woman
That every touch
That every feeling
All of its moments

Feeling of care
Love's surroundings
Held in each other's arms
True now?
True forever?
Love's trials
Succeed or fail
A chance taken

I walk the path
No task in mind
Walking the side of loneliness
Empty across from me
My life so empty
Until I found her
A love so true
So fair in beauty
A killer smile
To make you senile
Her presence said it all
Everything I could want
Everything I could ever dream
She opened the door to this broken heart
A love so sweet
She made my life complete

Broken down from there
That wasn't fair
Everything I had
Everything that I ever cherished
It all had perished

I found myself on that path once again
Yet with a task
Winning back her love
But I'm trapped
Nowhere to go
I wish she knew
What I've gone through for her
Losing her
Mentally and physically
She has lit a torch within
Torch that burns bright
Yearning for her body and love
To lose this love means the world
To lose it
A fear in never loving again
Love is funny
Love is time
Her love remains on my mind

I wish I could say the words
To have her presence in my life
I could sit here
Shed all these tears
Spew all these words of love and appreciation
Never changing a thing
I am not senile
A brother who loves a love
Wanting a certain love

LOST GIRLS

It's been about a month and I couldn't be any happier. It's funny though, after all this joy, I still question where I stand. I always imagine things that can never be, and compare that to which I have already. I guess that's how I measure happiness and I end up losing in the end. To be honest I have never found a girl that I have really been happy with in the past 6 years. I've had about ten relationships over this span and not one have I really cared about or showed any remote interest in. I just have not thought much of anything; they're all just forgotten memories. I've had a few one night stands and to be honest, I'm just sick of living the life of a bachelor. Not to be conceited, but a few have had interest in me; I just have not shown them the attention that they would appreciate.

Everyone is responsible for his or her actions to a certain extent, and I am one who can own up to any mistake that I have made. I met a few who were ready to pour out their hearts and souls to me because they fell in love. A few I have slept with, but they are just as guilty as I am. Make no mistake though, I respect them for feeling the way they do, but I can't be responsible for the emotion that is set upon me. If I'm not mistaken I'm used just as much as girls may think I use them. Some girls feel that if I sleep with them then the next day I'll fall in love but I'm sorry that's just not the way it works. I do have feelings for anyone whom I'm involved with but maybe not to the extent where I want to have a relationship. I don't mean to sound cold in anyway.

At times in life people want to play this game where it's every human for him or herself, and that's ok. Lies are very deceitful and it hurts people, and the word love usually comes into play; in most cases it creates mixed emotions and that's not fair. The word love is expressed to get into another's pants and that's just not the way it's supposed to go down.

SELENA

Hey Selena, I guess you haven't heard from me in a long time, since we separated five years ago. When we spoke on the phone you had a lot of questions that I left unanswered. I respect the anger and frustration that fills you within; after all I failed to call you after such a long period of time. I think I should let you know what you should've heard a very long time ago, what took place and what everything was all about to me. I think it's time you know the truth. When I was just about thirteen years of age I fell in love with a beauty like you. In a matter of a few short months we were able to express our love for each other, as well as utter the words I love you. We talked for countless hours on the phone and I can honestly say that since you I have not experienced anything half as great as the way we were. We embarked on dangerous territory because at some point I thought to myself what was love? I questioned it in every way and tried to figure out what it was. After five years I finally figured out what it was, except it's too late and you're gone; if I could change back the hands of time I would wish I never parted from you. Even when we see each other to this day we both are at a loss for words. A stare down occurs when we are around the same vicinity, and it's like flashbacks occur of our past. We both sense beautiful things of what we had and still can, but we both know that can't happen.

Honestly in all, there's not a day that does not go by that I don't envision you in my mind. Something that could have been and was meant to be but that's not the case is it? Over the past five years it was the picture of you that has allowed me never to fall in love again. Everything became about you, your smile, sweet lips, warm body, and the way you caressed my body like no other. I became lost in this world with no direction without you by my side. Selena, you were my heart and soul, my everything. I know that you are aware of how I feel because that's what was so special, we reminded each other of how much love we shared for one another. Perhaps I may never get over you, but I hope to look past you in experiencing love once again someday. By the way, I love you and I'll never forget you.

WHO AM I?

Who am I? All eyes on me; I reflect on myself for a moment or two, if you don't mind. I look no further than within me to find that trap door that leads me to this mystery. Many of you think that I sold out to you but to be honest it was never about that. While you were out trying to do what you got to do I was doing my own thing. As a matter a fact, fuck you! Haters never prosper!

I guess you thought that I slept with your girl while you were out; well you were wrong as much as she wanted I told her no! You know why, because I actually valued our friendship more than some pussy ass bitch, sorry for my profanity. Sorry to say that your choice of wives has not been too good as of late but I'm not mad, I respect your decision that's what comes along in a friendship. I could have slept with every single girl that you had and you damn well know it but I eased away because that's my job. I stuck by you through thick and thin, and you dare to question who I really am. I questioned your every decision but I learned from that one mistake where we had an altercation because of that. I'll tell you what, every time she turns around and hurts you I'll take a step back and let her break your heart while you're blinded by her beauty. Her very eyes are deceiving and it is them that has undressed you within and taken your soul. You've come too far, even I couldn't tell you who you were.

I've been called every deceiving name in the book from being a coward, loser, and basically just selling out everything I put my effort into. Don't get me wrong all that is understandable, respected because all that is your opinion based on my actions. It's funny that you can derive so much, but it's accepted. I never faulted anyone from speaking their mind, much less presenting their view on how they see things; after all I too love to ventilate my mind sometimes.

Now that all that is set aside and said and done with I got some things to say, don't tell me you thought I wasn't coming back, please give me a break let us all have our turn. Do me a favour, look at yourself in the mirror and tell me what you see? Ask yourself who you are? If you don't know who you are, how can you even fathom your dreams to come true? It must be difficult to smile knowing you don't know who you really are or even have some clue. On the other side of things, it is really difficult to know who you are going through the same exact things and experiences I've been through right? I think not, we came from the same place knowing what it was like to get here. If you ask me, you sold your soul; you're the coward who couldn't make it on your own and you dare question my integrity. You're not real; you're fake, just a poster image. Me, I'm the real deal, the truth. I represent everything I said I was and plan to be and if I don't then I'm only selling out myself, nobody else. In all I'm the truth; when I walk I represent me with my head high facing all odds.

I'M GONE

When we first met we both caught each other's eyes from across the room but I have to admit I never thought much of it. It became a thorn in my side and forced me to confront you. We talked over a period of time and hooked up at the movies as well as dinner. I guess you had your own perception of the situation; all I wanted was a friend but you obviously wanted more. I questioned it as we took it to the next level because I was always a difficult person who never knew what he wanted. As we proceeded on with this sexual thing we had, I began to wonder if it was really what you wanted or more. Though I continued to pound it into your head that all I wanted was a friendship between us, and if this jeopardized this whole sexual relationship, I wanted no part of it. You insisted though, that when I found someone else you would be able to accept it.

I found another who made me feel special, not that you didn't, but I felt that she was the direction I most wanted to follow. I think it was just that she had more to offer than you. You just were able to offer me everything except for conversation and an open ear, where on the other hand she offered that and a whole lot more. You questioned my decisions after you swore to refrain from doing so. I felt like you put me in this corner and threw this guilt act at me as if I were to blame for the emotions you felt for me. I'm sorry but I can't be responsible for what goes on within you. You threw this all on yourself. I'm partly to blame, but you've got to recognize the position you're in and realize if you want to accept it or not. I'm sorry it had to end like this.

At a point in life we are all faced with decisions that we must make. Though we may be placed in a corner we must learn to get out on our own by following our heart and dreams. You were everything but that gut feeling wasn't all there; it was just something felt deep within. She had that certain spark to her that was able to hold on to my heart. You had my heart and soul and still do, but it was that decision that I had made, though I would have wanted it with you. Anything is possible in this world; maybe it was the right decision, maybe not, I guess time will tell. They say if what you let go comes back to you, it is yours. Last but not least I love you.

Lost World

I woke up to it every morning, the annoying radios that refused to shut off, ringing in my ears of certain individuals, and an amazing teacher who convinced me to attend her class every day. Her smile which could ignite a fire, and of course her joyfulness that kept everyone around her in good spirit. I was surrounded with individuals, who only accepted perfection and if they did not achieve it, drove them into insanity. How about the miserable one who walked into class everyday crazed and confused. I felt some of them looked down upon me because I was never like them or I was never able to perform up to their capabilities. That's okay though, because I always disregarded their comments made towards me. Sorry I wasn't able to state my intellectual abilities as great as you, I don't believe that being better than you was ever an intention.

We live in a world where millions of people whom are imperfect walk the streets every day. Trying to be perfect is not a goal to set because it will never be reached, striving for excellence would be more realistic. If I could change my surroundings, I would give it up any day of the week. High on life is what I am because I have no other way of living my life. Every mistake drives you miserable, and it eats you up inside that you're not that brilliant being that you want to be. Accept what you are and not what you're not. Accepting yourself is what you failed to do, because that is not who you want to be. I accepted who I was a long time ago and never tried to change because of who others wanted me to be. I think we all face that at a young age; we face an identity crisis where we get stuck and become confused with others' perceptions.

My life is based on living it, getting through every day, and directing that remote towards the task at hand. Whoever told you that it wasn't all about that almighty dollar; then that was a bold-faced lie. It seems as though that's what controls the world, and superiors use that as their power to rule the world. I'm focused on getting the bills the President and Queen got their face on, and surviving. These days nothing matters anymore, people have no remorse, and people are dying for no apparent reason.

I never believed in a friend, I always thought I had enemies. I have acquaintances because the term friendship can never be described. Never had I had a true friend in my life and never will I, until I can be proven wrong that remains yet to be seen. Wow! I live in such an imperfect world where my surroundings continue to strive for perfection rather than success. I wonder if sometime in the future we can face reality.

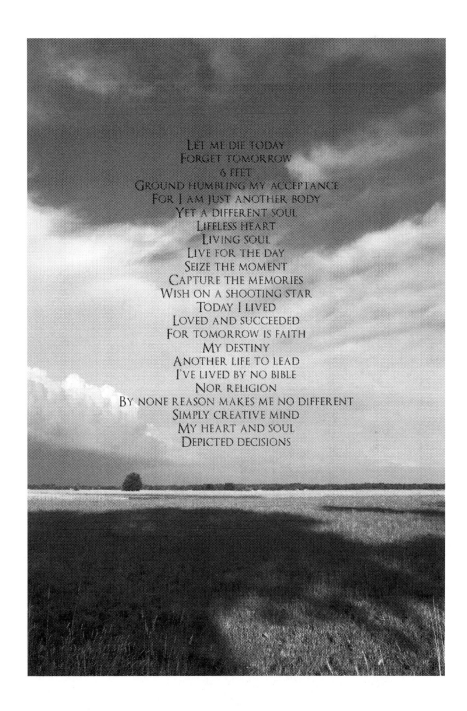

Let me die today
Forget tomorrow
6 feet
Ground humbling my acceptance
For I am just another body
Yet a different soul
Lifeless heart
Living soul
Live for the day
Seize the moment
Capture the memories
Wish on a shooting star
Today I lived
Loved and succeeded
For tomorrow is faith
My destiny
Another life to lead
I've lived by no bible
Nor religion
By none reason makes me no different
Simply creative mind
My heart and soul
Depicted decisions

CRITICS

I guess you all have had your overview of my perception towards a lot of things. I've been blessed with your suggestions on making this whole project of mine better. Little do you know, I asked what you thought of it, not how I could make it better; as if I need to sugar-coat my life and experiences. That is up to me to decide. You referred to suggestions and comments which you had about me, though it had nothing to do with the piece; damn you know nothing, it is you who I buck shots at. They wonder why I'm coming at them with this, they're not on my level, so I won't stop, and damn these fruits just don't get it.

Constructive criticism, I've received none because I seek nothing from anyone but myself. I felt that a lot of you refrained from giving your true honest opinion about this whole piece that I constructed. How about the one where they thought the narrator changed and felt that a closing piece be needed to sum this whole project up, how lame is that? Little did you know this is never ending, A Piece of Me is what it is; my life it's never ending, till I'm buried six feet below. All I asked was for all of you to be real, and still you have a hard time doing so. In all honesty, none of you can touch me; I've reached a height you cannot imagine, and quite frankly a level of no comparison. So many of my surroundings believed that they were superiors of some sort, and better than me because I hadn't taken a lot of things seriously. This is me, the guy who loves waking up every morning and breathing, showing up to the institution that has helped to mold him. The last few years have been so hard to cope through; the puddle of tears, the money will never be equal to love. That's not what I'm about, am I safe? Yes I am. Why? I'm alive, breathing and walking, and I have fingers to write this. My goal is not to be better than anyone but to be myself, unique separate from the many but not better. So don't get it twisted; I mean what I say and I take back nothing.

CRITICS PART 2

When I presented critics earlier, a lot of you took offence to remarks that I had made. Many felt that I said harsh things but that was just the reality of it. On the other hand, many of you seem to be inspired by what I said. I'm glad I inspired the many of you; even though I must admit that that was not my main intention or point that I was trying to get across.

Labelled as being a lost boy, selfish, blunt, and a defensive little child, I spurned everyone and acknowledged what he or she believes in is of no importance to me. I believe that sugar-coating is of no importance in regards to my writing and improvement in writing but that is not what I asked for in the beginning. I respect each and everyone's criticism even though it is you who fails to see the real picture. When I first started this, my only intention was to express the many issues that have plagued my mind for quite some time. Though now I'm going to take it to a personal level, and reveal things that you cannot begin to imagine that could take place in such a young boy's life. In this I will reveal who I am and what has driven me to believe in the things I express. Many things have led me to believe so much in life and accept what has happened to me, as well as learn from it, and tell the world that I've survived all this and will continue to strive to be of greatness. If anything has been spurned or looked down upon, then that's me and how it all transpired. It is for you to take for what it's worth and take what you want from it. Make no mistake; it isn't over because it's just the beginning. I am not going to call out names cause then it wouldn't be fair at all. What I will say is, pay close attention because this is the realness. This is simply freedom of expression and the way I saw life, lived life, and continue to learn from it every day of my life.

Psychologists would have a real field day with my ass in regards to many of the remarks I've made to critics. All of my people are waiting to hear my rant to the world that surrounds me. The truth is no one will ever understand who I am, who I was or who I've become. Though they may understand what I represent and gain acceptance. This takes place every day, but that's ok because I am not asking for any of that. What I ask for is to just simply read on and pay close attention to the life of the little boy in the hood and his trials and tribulations. Before I start this masterpiece I want to thank you all who have given your criticism you know who you are and to the rest who scorn me thanks, but no thanks.

LITTLE K

It all began on a dark and stormy night where nurses surrounded me while I made the entrance that many have made into this dark and confusing world. Just 15 minutes after my troubled sister arrived. Tears of joy hit the floor as my arrival had been longed for. The hugs and kisses planted all over expressed the love that each and every family member had for my sister and I. This must have been the only family reunion that stood out in my mind as one of the fondest memories that the family could look back on where hate never played a role.

Since the day of junior kindergarten it appeared I had the perfect family: mother, father, four other kids, excluding my sister and me. I remember the days so vividly; waking up every morning attempting to doze back asleep while both parents insisted that I awake because Care Bears and Teddy Ruxpin were beginning. We all rushed down the stairs around the corner our faces planted towards the television screen ready to enjoy the adventure that we were about to embark on. While on our adventure, our parents were in the kitchen cooking up some good old soul food breakfast. We always thought, "What will we be having this morning?" Plantain and bread, fried dumplings, banana flitters, or just some good old hot cornflakes whatever it was it was always scrumptious. "Breakfast is ready!" Or "breakfast deh round de table!" as my father spoke in his accent, as he attempted to speak like a Canadian though it never appeared to work. We all raced to the table blessing my father as we passed by and he would reply with a smile. We quickly wolfed down the food as it looked and tasted delicious. After all this, our parents dressed each and everyone one of us one by one with equal attention. That's what was so special-our bond with each other. Our school, Flemington Public School was just over the bridge, five minutes away from where we lived so it never took long for us to reach this learning centre filled with all of our friends. Another day at home for me, I hung out with friends at the park, playing games and attending school. A sign at the corner of our school stated visitors must report to the main office before entering school property. Growing up in a place where the government makes cut backs to save another dollar in efforts to build something of more importance to the community, it left us with no other alternative but to play basketball on that blue and white authority sign. At the left corner of the sign, a screw was pleading to tumble to the floor because of all the racket it had endured over the years. It must have been all the slam-dunk competitions that we had. This took place at recess every day. At the playground now it was whole a different thing because there were slides where the girls would play; little boys in the sand getting their clothes all mucky, and the big boys at the monkey bars where challenges were being issued out constantly. As we all went back to class from break so excited, it was time to settle down and commit to our studies.

FEAR

I have a lot of fears
Fears for which I shed tears
Fears I confront every day tearing me up in every way
Fear of dying tomorrow
The hearts filled with sorrow
Fear of losing a best friend
Continuing the trend
Fear of not conquering a dream
Causing me to scream
Fear of schizophrenia
Fear of that close one taking her life away
Not wanting to stay
Fear of losing half of me
Caused by a close death
Fear of being heart broken
Tearing me apart
Fear of losing this love so deep
Fear of my father awakening with no vision
Never witnessing a bright day
Fear of my mother getting drunk
Contributing to destroying her liver
Causing me to shiver
Fear of my brother
Falling victim to gang violence
Fear of failing in life
Fear of never seeing brighter light
All this
Strikes fear in my heart
Ripping me to bits and pieces
I feel all this trouble
I witness all this drama
I stand victim to all this pain
Yet I find the strength to go on
As if nothing seems wrong
I stand trying to figure out solutions
But I'm left in allusions
Yet I live on

Hoping for a brighter day
Hoping for the best
But I face this test
On getting over these fears
Coming at me with a steer
I realize that day is long ahead of me
Until then
I'll keep life
To the best of my ability
Taking whatever comes my way
Face it
This is I
My life
My fears
For which I shed tears
Through my childhood years
This is I

HOMEBOYS

It's been quite some time
Since your death
Yet we still mourn
Still shed tears
Not a day goes by
That a thought of you
Never comes to mind

There's a picture of you
Etched in my heart
Never to be torn apart
Brothers till the end
Though you put to sleep
Your soul laid to rest
Now you have peace
You're free
Free to watch over us
As we live life.

THE TRUTH

I guess the truth is out and all came back and hit me pretty hard, you most importantly. I manipulated the whole world into believing so much after switching my story time and time again; this could've all been avoided from the very start with just the truth. Yeah, the truth! Is that so hard? Apparently I displayed so. I made everyone around me look bad just to hide what I got over a long time ago, that I thought perished; I guess not.

Most importantly baby, I hurt you the most and that I will regret for the rest of my life even though you may not believe it. I couldn't imagine this whole situation would have such an effect on you. I should have opened up a long time ago but it didn't happen, and I don't regret it.

A long time ago I took a life that I was a part of and helped make which was so hard to do. I felt embarrassed, disgusted with myself, and this is just something that I felt uncomfortable discussing even though I loved you so much. It sounds so easy to say, but trust me it would have been so difficult. I swore to myself I would never open this up to anyone and so did she, she just trusted the wrong people. I would have hoped that no one would have ever found out about this and let it be forgotten, but that wasn't the case.

I don't feel good about myself in any way; as a matter a fact I'm disgusted because you're the one I supposedly loved, and this kind of shit you don't do to people you love. I sat there and watched you hurt over all of this and all it took was a couple words and this would have never happened and we could've lived happily ever after. I felt like I didn't deserve to live and should be wiped off the face of this earth. I stayed up till six this morning shedding tears of guilt and feeling the pain I put you through or even some of it. After all this one would think how could I live with myself, walk the streets with my head up; go on a year knowing the truth and haven't said a word, just lie after lie. To be honest, I thought to myself and I have come up with an answer, and that's just unacceptable on my behalf. I'm wrong in so many ways; you can imagine and I don't consider myself human, because a person like me would never have done this but it's all said and done, and I can't change a thing, if I could I would, but unfortunately I can't and I cannot accept that.

?

How could I leave u standing?
In a world all alone
To fend 4 itself
Drowning in your ocean
Full of tears
Weeping and moaning
Wondering when the truth may float by
Even stifle you
Sending a message

The ocean flowing waves
Hitting the shore with rage
Full of so many thoughts and ideas
Coming to mind
Waves hitting the banks in so many ways you can imagine
But blinded by the contamination
Filling within
Corrupting the oceans train of thought
Leaving the ocean lost

GIFT I HAVE NOT

HEART I HAVE SO MUCH

I WRITE FROM THIS MIND

THIS POETIC MIND

THIS POETIC MIND

BEAUTIFUL MIND

FULL OF MISCONCEPTION

NON-BELIEFS

JUDGEMENTAL IN MANY WAYS

JUST AS YOUR BODIES WILL DECAY

MY MIND NOT SO

As I think to myself at this point right now, that is the only secret that I've kept from you from such a long time ago. As for the rest of the world and my involvement in it, everything you've heard is the truth, nothing held back. It seems like the problems my life revolves around are the two who I love to some degree. I can't deny that I have love for them; I have shared something special with them, in that you cannot understand.

I've never cheated on you, everywhere I went talked about this wonderful girlfriend that I loved more than this world itself. Many got jealous and got sick of hearing about you, let me tell you. You are my pride and joy; what I live for and feed on for everything. You are my heart and soul. This whole thing could have been prevented a long time ago, but it wasn't and I have to accept that even though it's tough. I'm still the person I once was and always will be me because that's all I can be, me. The only difference is I'm cleansed of the truth I withheld for a long time; if it takes a lifetime to make this up to you then that's what I want to do. Even if this isn't what you want then tough luck for me, I blew my chance on love for the first time.

My character as it stands right now, not so different, everything I've said to you is the truth. I really feel this love I have for you so deeply you can't imagine. I put you through a lot of shit and fucked you over the worst ways possible and I'm deeply sorry from the bottom of my heart. Sorry doesn't mean much right now but I'm always going to be me, the one you love and cherish so much. Don't let this take away everything we have. Please, I beg of you. I'm always going to be that cocky, arrogant, ignorant, funny, fun loving individual that you fell in love with and I'm sure you want to see that. I don't know where your mindset is right now, whether it is with me or as far away from me as possible; that scares me so much right now. To be honest if you say goodbye today I'm going to disappear, separating myself from the world and the people within it; not dating for a while, no sex, nothing further than conversation. This is in no way meaning anything towards you; it's just that I'm lost without you and I feel that if I'm not with you then there is no point in being around here much.

In all honesty baby I want you forever and ever. I'm deeply sorry for all the pain I've caused you. Baby, I love you. All I want you to think about is all the good things we have over the bad even though I've hurt you so much. Just remember, I'm me, the guy you love and cherish so much, don't forget that. Don't say goodbye baby, just give me a hug and let me know we can get over this whole drama.

True Ties

I've learned that everything is done for a reason, and for those reasons you will never understand, that's fine with me. Everything that has been said on my behalf has been from the bottom of my heart, and if you can't respect that or even believe in it then that's okay I've done my part from day one. I must admit if this were to happen all over again even with my mistakes and all I would never take it back. It has enabled me to see the light; which has helped me to learn the true essence of life itself, and you, for one was worth it. But we're not meant to be together forever. I never lied about love, I really did cherish you. I don't think that you respected me enough to breathe on my own and you felt as if I needed you to lead me every step of the way. The truth is I really needed you but not in the way you imagined, wished, or even dreamed. I would never reveal what really went down that night because it was none of your business, nor did it concern you in any way. So you can consider that the answer in case you think that I would someday eventually tell you the truth.

OPEN UP

On again
It's the story that has been told
One true meaning that purpose
That pot of gold
Life we seek is destiny itself
In it for life itself
There it shall begin
Many lines have been written
Some even told
Others even testified and sworn upon
Many false, some even true
I am not writing with any purpose, just to rhyme
Merely just to provide thought and justice within oneself
Knowledge to the brain
In the intention you wish to contain
Knowledge is food for thought
You must have forgot
Go ahead recollect those memories
The many thoughts
As many answers
There are so many notes
Connect within
For there you shall begin
Speak now and speak forever
Everything you shall endeavour
Think of life and nothing in particular
Picture that major figure
Picture that picture
Envision whatever it is
Speak your mind etched in stone
Never to be forgotten
Blood flows the veins and pumps the many thoughts
With the intention to be caught
Feel not a vague of the rhymes
But all of the mentioned thoughts
Every word and the slightest thought
Never to be forgot

On again
It's the story has been told
Life itself shall unfold
One true meaning in mind, one thought
To get this message across

True Lies

The kid is at it again, walking the thin line because of his past once again. As a matter a fact it's more than that, I must admit. I've made a lot of mistakes time and time again I really don't know how you can put up with it, but wait isn't it love that's right love it is. That's the thing about love, no matter what happens, if you believe then giving up is not an option. We both see things in a different light, from a different perspective, but that's ok that's just normal we are both different just like colour. You can't expect me to see things the way you see it, what you can hope for is that I understand why you feel this way and what I can do to change it, and make you feel better. I never thought that a dance would mean much, but I guess I was wrong. For me to say that I'm going to never do it again, then you have to accept my word, not throw it away. I understand about this whole thing; about being completely sort of detailed about my day and what I do in it, I respect that, believe me. At this point I don't know what to think of myself because I'm the cause of all this (tears of frustration); now I feel like what's the point of continuing with this relationship, but that's love I guess. Problems come with the territory, problems that could have been avoided, but still they arose.

When this all started I distanced myself from the world, we both did and you know it. I did it because this love was unstoppable and nothing could get in our way. Yeah I didn't forget the other mistakes I made along the way. I gave up everything and now you dare question that you are not number one in my book that's not fair. How do you derive with all this, I find that disturbing. I can understand that we both do things differently. Love is learning experience and I'm not just saying that because I'm wrong; that's just reality, the things that you understand the first time I may not because we are different. Everywhere I go you are on my mind, whether it be pub night, school, and work or even walking down the street, you're just everything, my heart, my soul, my everything this is all you. If I really love you how could I purposely hurt you, that's not me.

The whole world will now have to surrender to you because you're worth it. Maybe this should have been done a long time ago but I never thought of it this way. I mean I distanced myself far enough, but that's not enough, I respect that. To make it clear I want to do this because its best for us, that being friends come and go but you being love comes once in a lifetime, and you will always be there. To me it's just another friend. I really understand what you mean about being more open and I can do that with another chance, that's funny I've used up a lot of those.

The way I think of life seems somewhat out of the ordinary, I mean the happy times fill me within despite all that has happened between us. Staying up late at night waiting, hoping that you would call just to say good night, to hear your voice utter the words I love you. Walking with you to work, then you closing your eyes and depositing an A close to your heart and touching it so gently. Sleeping with you naked, looking at my skin close to yours thinking the only thought that comes to mind, one word so powerful, forever. It seems that this is headed nowhere but down and I take full responsibility. I want you to know I'm deeply sorry. Damn, I'm crying as I write this. I swore I wouldn't do that. My world is coming to an end with you, I think not. Baby for every dark night comes a brighter day, and in our case this is we. I went to sleep at seven this morning thinking about you to myself in the dark; just wondering about everything, everything I put you through. It felt as if what happened still remains a thorn in your side that will never go away; maybe that's just me thinking, not a specialty of mine. I sat and thought about a lot and how everything happens, and what I do and I've learnt to accept a lot, believe me.

OTHER SIDE OF THINGS

I was always content on committing to whatever made you happy; with love sometimes comes the responsibility. Whatever it took to light that smile upon your face I did. I've shown the beautiful side as well the deep and dark side of things that took place in my life. The bad side comes out in us at times, and I must admit that sometimes we let the bad side get the best of us; of course you would lead by example in that position. You have said some deep and dark comments to tarnish my character as if I were some stranger you met the other day; it has also affected our relationship in a number of ways.

It's been said that I am a person of distinct character, hopeless and uncaring and last but not least, selfish. I am a person who is all about myself; everyone around me, I consider of no importance. In the past couple months I've been open to criticism of numerous characters, most importantly you. We say a lot of things when we feel that rage within us, and it gets the best and that is all a part of who we really are.

For the most part you have filled my heart of such joy that you can't begin to imagine, that you fail to even believe, along with key components such as support and guidance, and a shoulder to cry on. Since you have walked into my life I have witnessed brighter days. I've woken up every morning with a discreet smile on my face, and thanks to you, it's been carved in stone. Your heart I captured, as expected, which you so graciously appreciated.

Every bright day comes with glitch of darkness. You've shown me another side of you that I thought I could never witness. That caring and selfish kid who never gave an ounce about anyone, meaning you in particular, how could I be who you said I was. I broke your heart and left you alone to cry in that dark corner with the comfort of me knowing the truth. In all honesty I can't control who you are or what it is you want to be. I look back, that was not me. No one could understand what took place two years ago because you could not imagine what it was like in that predicament. I am sorry to an extent, but I am most definitely loyal to my people and most importantly my word. I not only withheld it from you but the world as well. This revelation is my side of the story, and like they say, there are two sides to every story. Being that inquisitive person, you always were craving every bit of detail that was my past, which I was patiently trying to leave behind but no matter what you found some way to bring it back to haunt me. This seems to be the most important issue we fail to discuss for what reason, only the man above knows.

The letter was written so it was said to be solid proof, so it was to be presumed. I'll say it again; I held it down for whoever was true to me since day one. You sniffed your way into an area where you were stifled; don't get me wrong, you deserve to know whatever it is I want to tell you. You seem to think that you were the decision maker in the relationship. Don't get it twisted, don't forget about me, it isn't all about you, or so you seem to think. After putting such great thought into it, I've grasped a slight idea of why it is the way you are: I've been through a couple girls, that's an understatement; you've just been that person who is contained and destined to know every single bit of detail down to the bone, and that is just you. This love that you have fallen into has driven you crazy and insane, and for some apparent reason you thought you had majority control over me. I thought I told you no dog could control me.

My past haunted me every day I had spent with you, wondering what I've done, what I haven't told you or what you may even find out even though it may not be that important. I found it so difficult to please you, even with the normal aspects, and that was not me. It just wasn't in me to commit to something like that. I think you expected a great deal out of me, and that I felt I couldn't deliver because your expectations were at an extreme. I walk through many days with the daunting task if trying to figure out what it is you wanted from me or of me? I woke every day with new expectations hovering above my head; pictures, and words painted upon my walls. This fed into my whole perception of love, the many tasks, ups and downs, and not to mention what it stands for. I still wait that day to find out what it is truly like to be in love.

9 Months

The saga dates back nine months
To where it all began in one's bedroom
Supposedly happening
The letter was written
So was the response to it
I was there taking part
Such an intimate night
The candle light at a swagger
Me with my dagger
I was there
She was there
To that I swear
No error was committed to my knowledge
You read the letter
True ties True lies
The kid is at it again
Continuing that trend of his
How devious such a plot
Done for a reason you fail to realize
I knew what leaked out
The many rumours and accusations
Some true, however
I know not the whole deal
Never did and never will
I never took that life alone
She was there
I was there for her
You're not there for me
Judging my character
I never knew
I knew her
She was herself
You were some stranger in my life
I cried for some reason to that I do not know
The end of me was near
I found myself again
That kid
That young boy

Who they grew to love and appreciate
Who grew to disintegrate
Back into himself
I was who I was once again
I found myself thanks to you
Thank you for nine months

JUST ANOTHER DAY

At this point in time I don't know where my life is taking me, whether it's to greater limits, or to extreme lows; I hope it's for the best. I don't know whether to be optimistic about a love I had or a love I have begun to love again. Should I be pessimistic about it? The streets haven't been too shy in expressing how they feel about the many choices I have made. I never doubted for one split second the way they felt. I felt like they would always throw negative shots at me whenever given the chance, it's just like them to throw shots at the man. A part of me yearns for this thing called love or I once had and the other senses. Tears forthcoming for the destruction of the many thoughts and dreams that can never seem to escape my memory.

I wish what was then could be now or even seem the least bit evident in another beautiful love. You exemplified everything love should be or even seemed to be, it seemed the closest thing to perfect. We planted a seed together and it grew as one, never drifting apart. A branch at one with its own sense of self, never frustrated by the wind, no matter how strong the current, and no matter how hard it rained. You set the bar, so to speak, of what love should aspire to be, I wish you were still around. What hurts the most is that you seem so close and not being able to hold you like I always did and forever always. I wish we could still be.

At times I could just think of you and that alone could cause me to smile ear to ear, just the thought of you causes me to blush. At times love can get so frustrating, no matter how much effort is put into it. I still cry at times thinking of what I once had with you; the beauty and very essence of what we shared spiritually, mentally, and physically. I remember when we use to walk to the corner shop with the crew. Lucky always told me I was a lucky man, and I always told him you were a gem amongst us all. We always held hands and shared passionate kisses. You told china you would rack her face if she ever made a move on me no matter what the circumstance and I believed it. Everyone uttered you two never get sick of each other and we kissed to that. We must have repeated the words I loved you a million times to each other and it was because we meant it.

There was no one in their right mind who could step to us, because it was the both of us they had top match and practically no one was having it, we weren't having it. Johnny said a lot about me to you, a lot that was true, somewhat yes, but for the most part he was attempting to tarnish my character, too bad all of that you knew before he opened his lips.

I took that summer break to myself to think about a lot of things that were taking place in my life at the time, a lot that you wouldn't understand or so I thought. You tried to reach me but I returned not one of your calls. I moved downtown to get away from the entire saga that was taking place and you knew a bit of how crazy it really was. While it remains fresh on my mind, as you always do as I awake every morning, let me tell you now what took place.

I really had no motivation that summer; all that I could think about was the green that was driving me every day. I was living for every day instead of the future. I heard how worried you were about me, believe me I had that on my mind all that time but it was just so hard to appreciate something so special at the time. You were the sun, moon, and stars in my life. I meant no harm in what I did but I did it for the best. I held it down downtown they respected me so much they thought I was some kind of god or something. A lot of girls attempted in the search for this charm of mine, but I told them that a girl back home had me in her pocket and that was that. My mother beat the hell out my father's girlfriend for some apparent reason as if she didn't have someone else on the side. I was in the midst of it all and it was so difficult to bear, I couldn't let you witness this deep pain that I had in me, it was just something I didn't want you do deal with. You had enough problems as it was with your parents.

I was free at a young age, free to play amongst the world with no guidance and protection. When you were inside with the reason of curfew I was out running the streets hustling cause that was the only thing I could do to get my mind off things, and ease the pain. No, not drugs, chocolates. I was running the streets a hundred miles per hour doing it all. The two brothers treated me like shit but it was the only thing that I had to do. When you're left with nothing much you just become accustomed to the bullshit that plagues your life. I lived in bullshit every day, the drugs, liquor and rumours that I had to put up with. Your mother's a feign, they told me; truth is I didn't even want to fathom the thought of her popping a vain, even using a pipe or even worse. It was just something I didn't even want to have in my head. I displaced all the rumours and beliefs, I played amongst myself, it just felt good having nothing look at, look forward to, even worry about.

We hit the bar every Friday night, playing pool, eating subs, pizzas, and hot subs my favourite; while he hustled, her too. I didn't know what to think of it, I was too young to take on so much, even though I knew so much more than everyone else. We took cabs downtown and ran them, a lot of nights through yards and over fences I was too young, fast and furious to be caught. The boys kept a good eye on you while I was gone for the two months and you never went anywhere; hoping, waiting for my arrival.

I came back first week of September and I saw you, the most beautiful girl I have ever seen. When I saw you it was as if no one else mattered, all I could see was the sweet complexion, caramel skin, and soft lips that I never had kissed yet. I was afraid to kiss you for some apparent reason until me and lucky made the bet and I did, and you became furious because of it, though you couldn't deny it, you fell in love with me weeks later. It was that one night we talked for about three hours, the conversation slowed down, and you told me you loved me. I was left in dismay, I had no idea how to respond to it, I had no idea how I felt about something of that magnitude, so I hung up the phone. You called back and asked what was wrong. I told you I feel this deep passion to forever want you more and more, and didn't know it that was love and we spoke about it. I told you that you were my soul and the reason for me waking up every morning. I then told you that you were brightest thing in my life that I loved so dearly. You were this person I put above all else, the only inspiration to go to school, my every thought, my every dream that I hope to have every night, the first thing I think of every morning, and last voice I fall asleep to at night. That night we spoke till 7 am and arrived at school late as usual, because we had to kiss each other good morning, every morning.

Before you attended gym class you had to kiss me and let me hold your jewellery because everything was safe with your chocolate sweetheart. There was never a day that I didn't walk you home. We walked under the bridge into darkness where we kissed and back into the sun where it always shined upon you. Through the courts and to our spot we sat and kissed for hours and talked about life and everything that was going on. It was so easy to speak my mind, and for you as well. There was something about the way you looked at me, and it wasn't because you grabbed my vision, but something I can't describe. I told you my deepest and darkest secrets that I never told anyone. There was something about the way you spoke to me, your tone, your voice, and voice of reason just captivated me and gave me to answers I needed. You were there when I cried my heart out; when I heard she hadn't arrived home yet, as well when he got busted and the feds tore the place apart. You did everything in your power to make me feel at home. You were always there to let me know that home was with you, and you would never leave my side.

I knew what I had with a beauty like you, but in the back of my mind I always told myself I never deserved anything as great as you because I felt I never appreciated something so special. Perhaps it's because I feel I have lost the most precious thing to me and that was family. They told me blood is thicker than water but that didn't seem the case. They never took me to what they consider my home, she cracked my head open, and it was as if I was in a coma, because I awoke the next day 27 hours later. She threw me down a flight of steps head first, and outside a second story window for some apparent reason. I have to repay my debt someway. To be brutally honest, she doesn't want it now cause I'm grown now and I don't think anyone wants it with me.

She ran up Marlee strip and popped off at a taxi driver for some reason, perhaps she was pissed drunk at the time, as always is the case, and it caused her to react in that fashion when asked to pay the fare which she committed to as soon as she step foot in that cab. Fast forward to this day if she wanted it with me I would give it to her raw. I heard she has no remorse, but the scary part is I have none either, I've been beating' up chumps since the beginning of time and she is just another chip on the block that I can chip off so if she knew what was best for herself she would stay away cause she doesn't want it with me. I say this out of anger and frustration but at the end of the day I love you to pieces and I don't want a war but truth be told I never backed down from one.

We boasted about who loved who more and we both never heard the end of that. I remember I use to call you back and tell you how much I loved you and before you had the chance to respond I hung up the phone and that was the end of the night. You tried to reply back but you weren't given the chance. I loved your style, your flow, and your scent when you walked in the room as well; when you eased the tension, whether it was between my troubled childhood and us. Chocolate is what you called me, sweet and brown chocolate delicious. You were sun in the morning walking down Highland Hill Road, brightest at mid-day walking across the soccer field, and my moon and stars at night when I slept to the sound of your voice. We loved each other as much as life itself. Your smile could ignite a fire, light a Christmas, you were my angel for consecutive Christmases, and most important, you knew how to make me smile. I don't think you could ever imagine how much I really did love you. I called you the other day because I was thinking of you and it was like we were strangers because you didn't remember very much, maybe because of him. They say love lasts a lifetime, I say eternity because it's never-ending and unforgettable. If it weren't for you I would've never known love or been able to pick myself up and do a lot of things. You reminded me about the beauty of life and why everything in it was so important to fight and live on. You taught me how to love in more ways than one. Above all else you taught me of the importance on how to be me, and never sell myself short and for that I am forever grateful. Senorita, last but not least I love you with all of me, my world, the world, I love you.

LOVE

Love not known at a young age but felt deep within. A search for what it truly meant, the deep passion two people shared, special bond, and most importantly affection. I too fell in love very young with one special beauty where it was apparent we were meant to be together. Forever is what we always dreamed and talked about. The understanding we had; the many agreements that never set us apart.

We were able to sit and talk for hours about life and the many things that were vital in us making it. Family life for the both of us was stable, not very wealthy, but able to survive. Married life is what we lived, we lived for each other, supported each one another, most important, we were there for each other.

At a school dance in late afternoon everyone is dancing having fun time. The DJ announces the last dance of the evening, so I panic and rush around to find a girl to dance with. I stumble upon a beauty who I ask to dance, as we begin to dance I start to feel this tingle, stars surrounding us, a connection unlike I've ever felt before. As the dance finished we walked off the floor holding hands with no attention towards it, staring into each other's eyes, for a supposed sign of hope for a tomorrow.

We were separated by race, as well as social group, due to the many stereotypes, and people who categorize others. A nerd who wore the same blue shirt, yellow dress, and a pair of church shoes, ridiculed everyday as she walked through the halls; and it never mattered to her because she was comfortable with who she was as a person. Negativity didn't result in a plummet, rather a rise.

THIS IS AN IMAGE
THIS IS NOT AN IMAGE
SO MANY THOUGHTS RUNNING THROUGH MY MIND
SO MANY THOUGHTS UNDEFINED
SO MANY THOUGHTS SEEM CONFINED
SO MANY THOUGHTS DEFINED
SO MANY THOUGHTS CONCEALED
SO MANY THOUGHTS COVERED
SO MANY THOUGHTS READY TO BE EXPOSED
SO MANY THOUGHTS OF INSPIRATION
SPOKEN IN EVERY WORD
SO MANY WORDS
SO MANY THOUGHTS
WHAT'S THE MEANING?

No Period

Thank God for giving me the gift
My life
I'll spew
To the very few
Who seek words
So talk about this
Talk about this indigenous plan
The little engine that could
Or the little boy that would
Everything that should
Come here son share my wings for you shall fly into the sunset
Hike then settle from dusk till dawn
Roast marshmallows under the moonlight fire tell jokes and scary stories,
That never linger in the back of my head
Watch the wind feed the fire
Feel the desire
I for one am such a liar
In the event of your demise
I must apologize forgive and forget that everything will be set according to
plan
Too bad you have no idea and can't understand
Cancer fills you within
What you lack is courage, respect, and dignity
You seem so content on seeing me before your bed
You may not get your piece of the pie
So many points intended I choose to share
What, you think this isn't fair?
You haven't come near
Feel this fear
Just a little of the wrath you received
Obviously no point intended indeed
Use her as an excuse no truth to that
This is a plot to hide the facts
And so much that you have locked
The little boy must go out and play
To this dismay
What he really lacks is fame and fortune

What he's left with is distortion
The playground full of kids
Many don't know what is really in front of them
But the reality they know is not reality itself
Not intelligent but they see a picture
Though it is faded
Things are tainted
Life isn't what it seems
But what it is meant to be
Though many fail to see

STILL FEEL ME

I want you to feel him, still feel him in every word, every response; this lisp that he speaks with, lisp that he speaks of, most important feel his wisdom, as well see his vision. I think he is a very passionate person who sometimes gets lost trying to fully express all the radiant emotions he holds. I think he is one of the rare who see love for what it is supposed to be, and that's why he has so much sorrow when he doesn't find it; when his partner doesn't wholly connect to him and understand. I think he has done more living and thinking, alone, at a young age than the majority of people he's encountered. He hasn't quite found all the answers he's looking for yet, but he's too smart and persistent to give up on his quest for knowledge and love.

Feel that raspy voice that is one of a kind, type that listens to no one, crossing the borders and guidelines. They said breathe with no voice, vent with no reason that you don't have a clue of, vent about what you've become accustomed to through your hood, where you grew up, the people whom you know. He listens to no one but himself, rebel of some sort, making his own rules, doing whatever it takes to attain whatever it is he wants in life. Is that right? Is it wrong? He becomes the judge and disciple to what goes down.

Air it out

Here I am giving my life to the public and not afraid to discuss it, all the stress and trauma that made me who I am. It became hard to laugh through, so many tears poured as if the faucet was left on. I walk this road with my past forever confronting me. Everywhere I go I see different people who want to take shots at me for some apparent reason, as if I haven't been through enough already. I'm forever walking with no destination in mind looking for something equally as important as my life itself, making sense of whatever it is I want to hold or consume. I don't know what it is that is in me but I hope to desperately find out. I feel like I need to confront my past with full ammunition head on and go at it with full force. It took me a minute to figure out I've become a man over the past few years, a boy before a baby. A childhood ruined by some sperm donor who had no balls to be a man; yet another man who had no reason to be there stood by through thick and thin. Watching that first basketball game, watch me run before I could even walk, throw as if I were some major league pitcher, first man to take me to the park, and pressure me to learn how to read when I didn't want to but had to; I bet you can't.

As I've grown up I've made my line of respect real thin, the people who claim to love and be my loved ones appear so distant. I have no love for so many people. Don't get it twisted, I'm not spurning anyone but if you think I am, I could care less. If offense is taken to anything that is written, then I guess I've gotten my message across if that applies to you, and you know whom you are. I've felt like the sun deserted me at times, refusing to shine over my life showing me the light when I was left in the dark. Even when my loved ones left me out to dry as if I were some stranger that appeared on their doorstep. Now I'm the key to the puzzle and everyone is beginning to realize that the most important necessity for everyone to be successful. I hold the key to that unlocked door that they seek so desperately to open.

I've held it down since day one, when it came to my family it only took a phone call and I was by their side, in return they took that and ran with it every time taking advantage of me. I was vulnerable at most times blood had always been thicker than water, until this day where it seems we have to choose sides and be at war instead being one even though the baby is here now. The new breed is born into a family of such confusion and animosity that everyone has in common. It feels as if destruction is just around the corner lurking like some thief in the night.

I'M GOING BACK

A few people seem to think I have nothing to say, nothing relevant to speak about or even write about. The truth is I have a lot on my mind and I feel this need to vent on what has transpired. They also seem to think they know what happened, raising assumptions or going by word of mouth. The kid did this, he did that, and he committed such a heinous act. A lot took place not too long ago on Blossomfield that made this kid into the man he has become today.

Take it back to yard where I use to wrestle with my brothers and sisters, with the imagination of a wrestler knowing how fake it was, mimicking all the movements, jumping off the top rope onto the planted body, hooking my opponent to the count of one, two, and three. We took turns winning; it was the only fair thing to do. We used a belt and a Frisbee in place of the championship belt. It felt like such an honour to hold the title. The wrestler I loved most was Bret the Hitman Hart because he emulated everything I was and everything I wanted to stay. He respected everyone around him; as well the most important thing in his life was his family. Even after that tragic day at the pay-per view when he was ripped off in the match between him and the Heart Break Kid, Shawn Michaels. I don't know what really took place but what I do know is he surrounded himself with family the tightest bond anyone would want to have.

I really envy those who have that big family; that was my wish every Christmas. I never believed in Santa but it was the spirit that the world had me accustomed to. I prayed to Lord Jesus Christ as well and asked him a lot of questions and he had an answer every time, in his own particular way. When they fought it disturbed me because I knew what was going on while my brothers and sisters stood in weary and had no clue what to do. Truth is, they could only do what they wanted and realized the seriousness of every situation. Parents just don't understand the power they have, and the capability they have even if nothing is done at all. Experience plays such an intricate part in a child's upbringing. Witnessing so much and going through so much has had such an effect on me growing up for one significant reason, being I still see it in my head all the time like a nagging flashback.

OFF THE RECORD

I sold chocolates at the age of ten and then on for a couple of years. That sweetness led me to acquire things such as shoes, clothes on my back when mom left. Dad left for a couple of months but he returned when he was booted, that faithful day that remains on my mind three women against one man. I witness that man bleed, sweat, and cry for what he believed in no matter the circumstance he was faced with. He knew the woman he fell in love with was out committing to something else. I solemnly swore to hold it down for them till the day I die. The truth is it's been such a struggle since day I was born, since the son was born, the good died young, and the bad got rich quick. The goodness left such a life behind. The assholes came and went, and whoever she was she displayed it by committing such cruelty to her own blood. My mind goes back and forth remembering what I have already vented about, but that's just me I can't forget but I can make the best of what's happened to me.

I woke up every morning to the sink and a toothbrush and him outside at all hours of the morning in that cloud of smoke awakening hours later to the same, it became that trend that he'd become accustomed to. The neighbourhood boys came through to do the same as if they all never grasped the idea of sleep. I seen that china white and pink pistol, it was all down for those dollars. He walked with the pistol most of the time and you would have never known. He saved my life in short court that day. I was surrounded by four of them, but it was okay when he arrived on the balcony. Wilson strip would have never been the same, had things gone another way that day. Life was a hustle to us all and it still is but it's how you go about your hustle. China white will run out one day and so will luck, it doesn't continue forever. The streets are always going to be there but it's what you make of it. It seems like the ghetto has a mental telepathy but I haven't fallen just yet but all the others have. Here I walk, wanting to create a trend but no one seems to want. On Wilson strip it was as if I had bounty on my head, my heart was always open to whoever wanted it. With me, I was only a pair of laces away and they knew it. I never ran from them, afraid of no confrontation, he who fears death is in denial. I know when my day comes I'll be gone, however forget not the fact that I'm here and I enjoy my struggle though it gets hectic at times I'm still here. I've enjoyed the death threats everywhere, I been chased with blades, chased by the cars, I still breathe this confusing breath of air.

To the goodfellas, nothing seems a distant memory anymore. Seems like it was just yesterday when we popped so many Christmas bulbs in the Jewish area and Italian strip and watched as the smoke arose from the depths of concrete, it sent a chill through my body. Running from the cops those Halloween nights, escaping the hands of young bloods that wanted to deprive us of our wealth that we so graciously earned; Jungle city seemed like such a goldfield, so much to find and seek, full of opportunity. I loved the fights we got into; it was warfare in the Jewish area, whoever wanted a price they got it. I love my home and I'll never forget it. Don't get it twisted. Circle B, Under Bridge, Over Bridge, Red Stop Signs and Yellow Lines I'm home.

REAL TALK

I felt like I've been real ever since day one and I have and forever will be down. If you don't believe me ask every member of the fabulous five. I may have lost myself a few times, but then again who doesn't. I never forgot who I was at anytime; I always knew where home was. I'm contradicting myself when I say I never believed in a friend; truth is I feel like everyone swearing to be down with me has deserted me and left me in that dark room to confide amongst myself. I've become so used to being forgotten, it's as if it's my normality now and it is I. I still have love for so many people that have left me in the worst of times. I was left in the arms of a stranger, where it was not left in his job description.

I heard you told her to leave after you committed to lying in bed with her and creating that inconspicuous egg that eventually hatched. You told her to walk away from that situation at the moment in time, and you consider yourself a man? You left me alone in the world to roam, to walk the streets. Though it didn't quite play out like that, that would be the case in any young boy's mind. Then again, he was there for me through thick and thin taking his rightful throne, a king in my mind.

Joey put a knife to my throat and threatened my life a couple years ago, and Petty and Pablo held bottles to me ready to crack my skull open all over a game of basketball. I beat four guys to a game of eleven even when I spotted them nine points and took a beating doing it. Going through that doesn't prove that I am a soldier in any form, but it shows that I became a man, a real man without that unknown donor. I raised hell before I spoke softly I was quick tempered they say and I think I am. If I saw you tomorrow and you even began to utter certain words, I think we know what would happen. I'm six-foot-two, a hundred a seventy-five pounds; I don't think you would stand a chance. We spoke briefly not too long ago and I had a choice of words that you didn't appreciate, but then again that's what happens after twenty years, then assuming your rightful position.

I saw Joey a week later and we hit it off again one on one but nothing came about. I could see the fear in his eye; the fear of leaving with a bloody nose and a busted lip would have been the case I think he saw it flash before his very eyes. After all, jungle city is my home; I never learned anything while I was there. I paid my dues, I made the news, and I mean the real six o'clock news - playing in my home of Maple Leaf Gardens; this is hockey city after all. Just ask Charlie; Jabbo, Toronto's finest, tattooed on his arm, or even ask Killa who's beaten my ass enough but still remained my brother through these years. We must have fought over fifty times and over nothing; that's just what we did to have fun. We've been fighting all our lives, that's just what we did best. I know nothing better than a good old scrap. However, that was then, I'm not a changed man but I know how to fight without my fists, as well as with this mind that I've been blessed with.

I was there at the centre when the train came through and held the light skin kid up for fifty measly dollars, it's amazing how we all swore we were brothers but the power of that almighty dollar always became that mighty downfall. Fox was shot two times I believe, I remember the shots vaguely. I was walking home at the time, and it was like it was a normal day. I'd heard gunshots before; it was no nightmare, even at the age of ten. I never forgot much it still remains instilled in my mind. A lot of people claim bird to be an informant, as well as sparks, brothers to some extent. Who knows who said what while in the presence of the blue authority. I will not refer to them as pigs because to some degree they help keep the streets safe.

I met up with Joey this past year in the alley and I was going to explode but he had his back protected well by him and his brother. My brother however had his own way of dealing with matters. The strip would have been the same had Joey made a few different choices. Pellets move faster than a fist and they make a hell of a statement. I could always fight a war at any degree but that wasn't in my place. My war is at one with myself with this pen and pad dictating reality and how I saw it to be. Joey couldn't speak with the barrel in his mouth so he had to shut it. When he spots me to this day we are not friends, but bad blood still exists. My life has been threatened so many times; it's as if it's become an everyday occurrence. There are a lot of guys who would love for nothing more to find his body in some ditch parked up full of led, but I don't wish death upon any man. In that I say to any living organism that wants me dead, label me, call me, and try to desecrate me. I know any man is capable of making it happen, I don't run with the city boys, but they run for me.

LIFE

THE ONLY LIFE I KNOW

NO REGRET

NO FEAR

PERSEVERE OR FAIL

INNER REFLECTION

OUTER REFLECTION

MY HEART

MY SOUL

THIS LIFE IS MINE

I've lived life
I've suffered
I've been through fire
I've been back

Many things I've surpassed
Many yet to grasp
Many things seen
Many I have not
I've bled
I've felt pain
I've cried
I've been down

I am but beneath you
Nothing more
I lay there
Bottomless pit
Hovered over me

Nothing but dirt
Your vision
Nothing but despise
Your feeling

Never fear
For I lay
Dead beneath you
For you to crowd
Your head such evil thoughts

My heart, which is broken
My soul, which you have taken
You have taken half of me
Which you cannot see
My love for you is deep
That you did sweep
Your love I cherished
It has perished
Your love I adore
That you ignore
Our life together
Is just a feather
That blew away
And didn't stay
It took its place
In holy grace
Never to return
Now adjourned

Life
The only life I know
No regret
No fear
Persevere or fail

Inner reflection
Outer reflection
My heart
My soul
This life is mine

Feel my pain
See my struggle
This is my life
So you see

Feel my footsteps
Feel my heart beat
Can you hear my heartbeat?
Can you hear my footsteps?
Can you be me?

Can you look into my eyes?
Like open doors
Can you open the locket to my heart?
Like turning the knob

Can you wake me up inside?
Awakened by your love
Can you kiss me?
Can you hold me?

Can you make it through my core?
Awaken my inner spirit
Can you save it?
As if it were dead?

Can you breathe love within me?
Can you touch me inside?
Can you see within me?
Can you save me?
Above all else
Can you love me?

Walk with me
Take some time and walk with me
Take a tour with me
Take a walk into my past
Take a look at the present

Many feel the presence
Feel the fear
Feel my heart beat
The tears sweat inside
I hide so much

Walk with me
Take some time and walk with me
Take a tour with me
Take a walk into my past
Take a look at the present

Can you see what I see?
Feel everything I feel in this world?
Is everyone a snake?
Or is there some motive to everything?
Is everything for purpose?

Walk with me
Take some time and walk with me
Take a tour with me
Take a walk into my past
Take a look at the present

Take a walk into this voyage of mine
Realize why I think everyone isn't so kind
Realize why people are so hateful
So ungrateful
What's in everyone's best interest
Is what I manifest
I live for

Walk with me
Take some time and walk with me
Take a tour with me
Take a walk into my past
Take a look at the present

What is this so called life?
What is loyalty?
I don't recall ever noting the definition
I don't know what's real anymore

Walk with me
Take some time and walk with me
Take a tour with me
Take a tour with me
Take a walk into my past
Take a look at the present
Was that so hard?

Gift I have not
Heart I have so much
I write from this mind
The poetics of mine
This poetic mind
Beautiful mind
Full of misconception
Non-beliefs
Judgemental in many ways
Just as your bodies will decay
My mind not so

I'VE LIVED LIFE
I'VE SUFFERED
I'VE BEEN THROUGH FIRE
I'VE BEEN BACK

MANY THINGS I'VE SURPASSED
MANY YET TO GRASP
MANY THINGS SEEN
MANY I HAVE NOT
I'VE BLED
I'VE FELT PAIN
I'VE CRIED
I'VE BEEN DOWN

Love is so precious
So beautiful
So hard to find
So divine
Quench my thirst
Fill my hunger
Be my last breath
My loss for words
Fill my heart
Be my deep soul

Come within
Feel the pain
I ask one thing
Be a part of me

Come back?
I never left
You did
My heart's been there
Been back

My heart you held once before
So preciously tight
So gentle
So secure
Forever?

Not the case
So I thought
Come back?
I never left
You did
My heart did
Long ago

To the thugs
Hold your head
Stay strong
Life can last but a second

Guns, whips and chains
Is no life
Dying for your hood
Nothing nice

Slugs determine realness
Real then separated from the fake
A genuine thug
Strapped without forgiveness
No heart
Breathes so much pain
Inflicted upon others

No love
Bitterness built within
Driven by that dollar
Not an inch of power
No control
With need of someone to hold

The world breathes
Such jealousy and envy
Doors closed
Trust, never such a thing existed
The world
A thug's world

I have so much to say
Open your ears
Listen attentively
I beg of you
But a second of your time

Read along
Figure the message
Hidden between the lines
This no rhyme

Read it
See it
Believe it
Right before your very eyes

I was such a little soul
Seeking the guidance and support
Never ended up before that very court
Stuck in the system
That life I chose never lead

I've never copped a plea
Nor expected any bargain of any sort
Never released any slugs
Never carved

Never seen the bars
Confined to a small space
Surrounded by drug dealers and killers

I am but a little soul
Under guidance
Never ended up before that very court
Stuck in the system
That life I chose never to lead

All about the rep
Yet you took one extra step
Closer to death
Testing this so called faith
Which you think you have so much

Life yet not based upon faith
But upon how you live
Roads chosen
Paths decided to walk
Journeys beckoned upon
Stars nearing closer
Closer and closer
Yet with blood sweat and tears
Still unable

Today
Yet such a special day
Not yesterday
The day before yesterday
Today

Yesterday
Yet such a beautiful day
Not tomorrow's day
Nor the day after tomorrow's day
Yesterday

Tomorrow,
Yet filled with so much love
Not today, nor yesterday
Tomorrow breathes love in the air

Today, yet such a special day
Yesterday, yet such a beautiful day
Tomorrow, yet so much love
Today, yesterday, and tomorrow

Lord above earth
In the sky
Where blue placates
Hidden amongst the clouds
Your wrath
Thunder and lightning
Heavy storm
Thumping the earth
As if we sinned

Morning a new day
You shed light on a new day
As it arrives
Perhaps a sign of better to come
Happiness fills the air
Breaths of hope
Dreams floating
Wind blowing
Sky blue as ever

Sun slowly falls
Light begins to slowly fade
Darkness is yet to fall
The moon is eminent
As it spreads its love
Bright night
Bright day
Now we must pray

I never had a father
Left a fatherless child
A bastard so to say
A mother alone
Nonetheless another statistic

Slain, not my heritage
Nevertheless my heart
My soul
Undying pain
Yet an urge to love
A father figure

Nonetheless a man I am
Man I've become
Inside me
I built in me
A beating heart
Repeated pounds
Love and survival
Honour and respect
To thy mother
To thy father

SOUL SEARCHING
SO DESTINED TO FIND
THIS TRUE LIFE OF MINE
EVERYTHING THAT FILLS MY HEART AND SOUL WITHIN
THE LOVE ONCE KNOWN
TRUE LOVE ONCE A GIFT
LOVE SO MUCH CHERISHED
LOVE SO MUCH YEARNED FOR
LOVE ONCE TO DIE FOR
DEEPER THAN THE OCEAN ITSELF
BEYOND HEIGHTS OF THE VERY SKY
SEEN THROUGH THE CLOUDIEST SKY
EVERY INCH OF ME
MY BLOOD SWEAT AND TEARS
I POUR OUT EVERY INCH OF MY SOUL
TO HEAR YOUR VERY VOICE
SUCH WARMTH TO MY CORE

My love knows no limit
Beauty of it
How it feels
Infatuated by the light
Its warmth
Burning desire
For its very existence

All alone
No one to confide in
When I sleep
When I wake

People pass through me, up, and around me
Over topple me
I am but a ghost
Ghost of bright light
Ghost of dark night

Who am I?
Can you see me?
Do I bleed?
Do I feel pain?
Can I just maybe
Just maybe, if possible die?
Am I like the rest?
What is it you presume?

Lost and so confused
To many
So many thoughts running through this thick skull of mine
So difficult to define
Too hard to decipher

Many thoughts contemplated
So many decisions to decide
So little time
I am but at mercy
A bottomless pit
Dirt filled to the chin
Smell and filled with such dirt inside to out
Left without a route

So near and dear to my precious heart
I'm looking to find my one true love
I'm waiting for you
I spend every day wishing for you
To walk into my life

Will I ever fully be complete?
For the love I have to share
So much care
It means so much to find you
Endure all the heartache and pain of love

I've been all around
Waiting for you
Wishing for you
Looking for you
Searched here and there
So little time to spare
I want it all
You

So many fans
The powerful media
So much of an effect on the world
If everyone knew the truth

What is home?
So many blocks corrupted
Filled with such evil
Single mothers
Kids running into the streets
Kids running for their streets
So much envy built towards supporting the blocks and projects

So much of the dollars to support the guns
So little to the schools
This thing we call culture
Whatever it is and composed
Society and media destroy the people as a whole
People the main objective
Or thought to be
Where's the justice?
Where's the love?
Filled with such warfare

People have no rest
Forever weary they are
Wondering to hear the next siren
Blue and red lights surround

On the streets they pray for better days
When the block would be worry free
Needles flooding the floors
Getting chased by the lights
Ridding of all the fights
Sleeping to such cold and dark nights
I pray and wish for better days

To my people
For my people
We are not oppressed
Yet filled with so much opportunity
So much to seek
Too much to find
Indeed we have the guidance

We have heart and soul
Willpower so strong
To withstand any obstacle
We fall
Leap right back
Face to face

To my people
For my people
We are but equal
Separated by colour, race, and collar
But we exist
With that we can't resist

Only the sky can be that limit
To reach and capture that entity
To fill that emptiness missing
It is hidden amongst the clouds
Difficult to find
But possible to reach

To my people
For my people
For we are but oppressed
With that find that nest
Hidden amongst the clouds

Can you feel my pain?
It burns so deep
The fire within
This burning blaze
Hurts so much
You have not the slightest clue

Feed not off my fire
It burns with a destructible desire
Smoke contaminating your lungs
Choking, coughing
A wish for a fresh breath of air
If you only knew how it could tear
Tears me apart within
I can't give in

I have so much fight
In the deepest of nights
Though so bright
This fire burns such a blaze
So much courage, faith and love
Deep within my core
I have not the slightest bit of death in me
If you could only see

I been down without you
I can't sleep at night
Holding my pillow so late
Never so laid back
My mind has such an attack
Filled with such empty thoughts
Mindless in such ways
No pictures
Vivid thoughts jump at me
Blinded, I see nothing

I don't want to be alone
Alone without you
Full of such content
My heart will not plummet
For I am filled with such care within
This deep love
I share for you
One day you will see
As if bright light
Has shunned your deep blue eyes

I can do it
If you want it
I can do it
Your dreams and deepest fantasy
I can reach your deepest core
Touch you
Stroke you over and over
Over again

Put you in the mood
Don't get too confused
Believe me I can be very crude
Your clothes, just lose them
Take them off fast or slow
Strip if necessary
I can be unnecessary

I can reach your utmost peak
Just let me seek
Touch your heart
Cause you to yearn for more
No questions, it's your way
I'm here to stay

Seek your spot
Believe me it'll get hot
From your neck
Down your spine
Oh you're so mine
I can be kind
So gentle
Rough and tough
Baby so hard

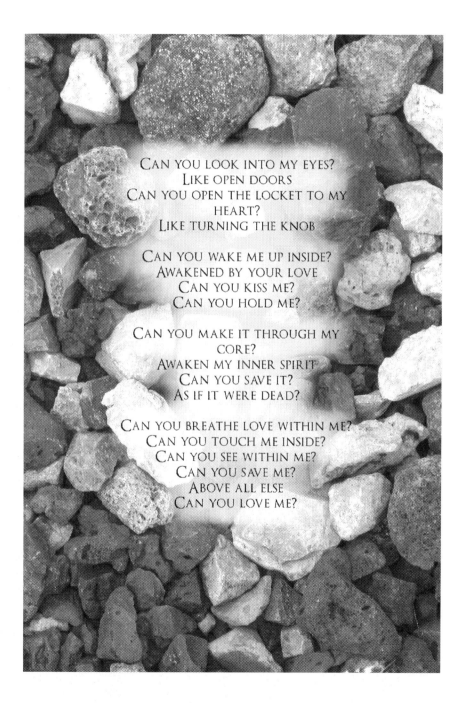

Can you look into my eyes?
Like open doors
Can you open the locket to my
heart?
Like turning the knob

Can you wake me up inside?
Awakened by your love
Can you kiss me?
Can you hold me?

Can you make it through my
core?
Awaken my inner spirit
Can you save it?
As if it were dead?

Can you breathe love within me?
Can you touch me inside?
Can you see within me?
Can you save me?
Above all else
Can you love me?

It's easy to look at my life
And see no pain
Switching from lane to lane
You could never understand this pain
It drives me so insane
This pain hurts so deep
My core cannot withstand
At times I thought I was the man

It's easy to look at my life
An see no frustration
So many breathes of frustration
Driving me so crazy inside
Feelings of such hatred within
Waiting to burst onto the world
Most times I sit and curl

It's easy to look at my life
And see no mind
For which you have the trouble to define
You have no idea
At times I feel as though it isn't even mine
Most times I see between the lines
People so unkind

It's easy to look at my life
And see no pain
Sense the frustration that builds within
Yet see no mind so out of control
Someday I may unfold

Sick and tired of the one night stands
Disgusted in you, you, and you wanting me to be your man
Stop fooling with my mind
Your love you can't define
My love you cannot obtain
This isn't a gift from god
I've come too far to have my heart broken
My love cannot be bought
Just a thought
There is a way
Pitch the realness
Hide not in closed closets
Behind closed doors
Keep it real
You be you
I be me
Then you may see

The essence of beauty
I cannot describe
It remains a thought on my mind
But if I must try
To explain a piece of the pie

Kind sweet gestures
A warm hug
A kiss to touch your spine
And make your soul quiver
A presence felt in the room
The smell of sweet perfume

The sweet in your tea
Causing you to plea
The twisting knot in your stomach
Causing your heart to plummet
Beat at vast speeds
She is one of your biggest needs

The essence of beauty
I cannot describe
It remains a thought on my mind

Cry me a river
Full of tears
Flooding the streets
Pouring through the cracks
Filling the sewers cracking the pipes
Smashing car windows

Feel my pain
Witness my misery
You can never see
How much my heart pleas

Inside my mind
So hard to define
I try to find a place of rest
This continues to remain a test
So many thoughts unexplained
Awake I am
Awake I feel not
Trapped in a maze
Which sometimes I feel is a phase

I suffered many years
Shed so many tears
Cry me a river
Watch me shiver
I'm lost in weary
Forever query
Light me a match
Lead the way
For I've been led astray

My destiny is living well
But feels within hell
My every step is calculated
For I feel as though I haven't made it

Shed so many tears
For times the end seems near
Living this life of pain
Feeling of nothing to gain
Visions of leaving this world in a hearse
My life seems cursed

Such a struggle to survive
If only I had some guide
I don't want to see the chalk lines
For I have been given that sign
I don't want to suffer no more

My life, full of so many bad decisions
So indecisive so unpredictable
Sometimes inexplicable
What's it like,
To be in love?

Something I can't buy
Many moments feel like the wrong time
But I want to climb
That love mountain
Though I cannot find it
Where does this life go for me?
I can't even fathom to see
I'm slowly finding out
What it's all about
I feel like I'm going mad
Feelings for one I once had
My heart is open to seek and find
Waiting for something to come to mind
Something to be mine
Just one of a kind is all I hope
I wish I could see through the microscope

Open my mind
Open my heart
Cease my soul
It's ready to unfold
I feel left out in the cold

Take me in
Let it all begin
I feel like this is a sin
Please get under my skin
I'm ready to win

Lose it all
Let it all fall
Your clothes to the floor
What's the score?
Your shirt your pants
Let me get a glance
What a sight to see
This body to be
Mine, yours, so what's the score?
I want more

So beautiful
So divine
Let me creep your spine
This love isn't one of kind
Just one to be mine
Unlike like no other
Yours to discover
Not a chance
You get but a glance
Beauty is sensuous
So voluptuous
A kiss to touch your heart
Cleanse your soul

Open my mind
Open my heart
Cease my soul
It's ready to unfold
I feel left out in the cold

You bleed just like me
Cry just like me
You see not what I see
Nor be what I want to be

The sky not my limit
Nor is there a mountain that I want to climb
Nor is there a ladder of success
Though I do get depressed

This is real life
My life right in front of me
I can't fathom to see the future
Though I do hope bright
I have no sight but vision
Dream so to say
With that I must pay
My dues, hard times and tribulations
In order to succeed

So repeat
Repeat I must
To gain that trust
Trust in my heart and soul
To reach my goal
I care not about the sky
Nor these high mountains
You see not what I see
Nor where I want to be

Remember back in the days
Take a trip down memory lane
Life so was so insane
The many times we tried to pull weight
Barely enough to feed ourselves
We were two soldiers
Two soldiers at one with ourselves
We were all about us

Remember all the cowards
So fake to themselves
Always wanting to spar
They swear they were stars

The time we ran from the cops
Through the fields jumping the fences
We swore it was the trenches
Not to mention
All the girls drooling
We were inseparable
Troopers
Just trying to live

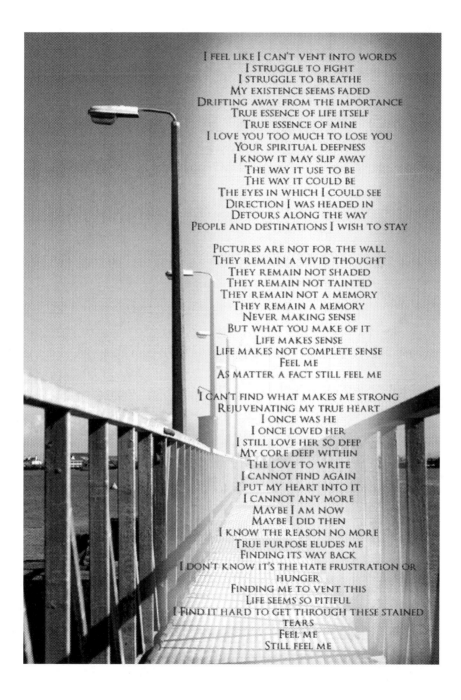

I FEEL LIKE I CAN'T VENT INTO WORDS
I STRUGGLE TO FIGHT
I STRUGGLE TO BREATHE
MY EXISTENCE SEEMS FADED
DRIFTING AWAY FROM THE IMPORTANCE
TRUE ESSENCE OF LIFE ITSELF
TRUE ESSENCE OF MINE
I LOVE YOU TOO MUCH TO LOSE YOU
YOUR SPIRITUAL DEEPNESS
I KNOW IT MAY SLIP AWAY
THE WAY IT USE TO BE
THE WAY IT COULD BE
THE EYES IN WHICH I COULD SEE
DIRECTION I WAS HEADED IN
DETOURS ALONG THE WAY
PEOPLE AND DESTINATIONS I WISH TO STAY

PICTURES ARE NOT FOR THE WALL
THEY REMAIN A VIVID THOUGHT
THEY REMAIN NOT SHADED
THEY REMAIN NOT TAINTED
THEY REMAIN NOT A MEMORY
THEY REMAIN A MEMORY
NEVER MAKING SENSE
BUT WHAT YOU MAKE OF IT
LIFE MAKES SENSE
LIFE MAKES NOT COMPLETE SENSE
FEEL ME
AS MATTER A FACT STILL FEEL ME

I CAN'T FIND WHAT MAKES ME STRONG
REJUVENATING MY TRUE HEART
I ONCE WAS HE
I ONCE LOVED HER
I STILL LOVE HER SO DEEP
MY CORE DEEP WITHIN
THE LOVE TO WRITE
I CANNOT FIND AGAIN
I PUT MY HEART INTO IT
I CANNOT ANY MORE
MAYBE I AM NOW
MAYBE I DID THEN
I KNOW THE REASON NO MORE
TRUE PURPOSE ELUDES ME
FINDING ITS WAY BACK
I DON'T KNOW IT'S THE HATE FRUSTRATION OR
HUNGER
FINDING ME TO VENT THIS
LIFE SEEMS SO PITIFUL
I FIND IT HARD TO GET THROUGH THESE STAINED
TEARS
FEEL ME
STILL FEEL ME

I'm not a mime
I don't read between the lines
Can't you understand this life of mine
Almost caught a brain tumour
Trying to escape the rumours
I am but one soul
So many intentions
Not to mention
Stop making me the centre of attention

I am what you will never understand
Never be understood
Yet generalized or categorized
Please don't apologize
Better yet wish for my demise
I am everything but an angel

All the denials
So many apologies
None accepted
So many disrespected
No point intended

So many names claimed
You swore to key to my fame
I hit the zone
Week in week out
You're nowhere about
I'm a soldier a trooper
I never thought I knew you
Make no mistake this isn't for you
I introduced myself to this world

I'm at odds trying to escape my grave
The sight to which I lay dead
So many dreams
So many nightmares
I don't know how my life will be
How will it end?

Let me write
I want to write
If I may repent
Let me repent
Let me speak
I want to speak
Let my voice be heard
I want to be heard
Let my actions be seen
Let me be seen
Let me cry
Do not dry my tears
Let me bleed
I don't want to bleed
Let me die
For I was born to

I have so much heart
A heart that burns for that abundance of success
Yet the streets have me oppressed
The authority figures think they know everything
Yet they know not a thing
So much knowledge
So brilliant minded, yet no heart
They see within their eyes
Discouraging my thoughts
Crushing my dreams
No provision of hope
Lacking that guidance and support
Providing no experience

I've seen it in my eyes
Been through the hell and storm
That became my norm
I've been through the pain and suffering
You have no idea
Fathom to even think my life
You would not have such a clue

My life always at odds
Never defying God
So confused all these years
Through the many tears
I grew up from being a boy
To what I am now a man
Never receiving it well
Never choosing this life
But this life chose me

The rumours have been obsessed with me
No matter where I went
The time spent
I've been through it all
I've had my share of falls
Ups and downs
My life's been turned around
Taken its twist and turns
Flips, so many I can't recall
My life has come to a straight stall
So many denials
So many regrets
So many hard pills to swallow
My life was once shallow

Mind, reality, and dreams
So hard to separate
The difference between them
The unsettled differences
The story behind everything
So called untold tale about two who were in love
Never ending within each other's heart
Destined to cross paths once again
The time has come within the dreams
The constant reminders come to mind
Reality needs to be written
For it once was
And someday again forever

Make no mistake about it
Any block can be laid to rest
For that matter put to sleep
It can rain
It can pour rain
Blood leaves a stain
Thicker than water
A bullet can change a life
Face imprinted on tomorrow's paper
Making the headlines

My best friend
My companion
I've never been hit
Never been broke
Attached is that lens, that scope
Special view to your heart
Detecting fear and hurt
Bottling up all that blood within
Seizing every single breath in you

We've been here before
Never been hit
Info red dot point blank
He has no heart
The devil corrupts his pity soul
Blood flows through the vein
Like no one else
He breathes not a single breath of air
He smokes leaving traces
Destination elsewhere
Hell or heaven

He plays his position
Sometimes the best of company
That secret stash
He feels the heat
Before it arrives
His slender body
Shine as chrome
Never wanting to leave home

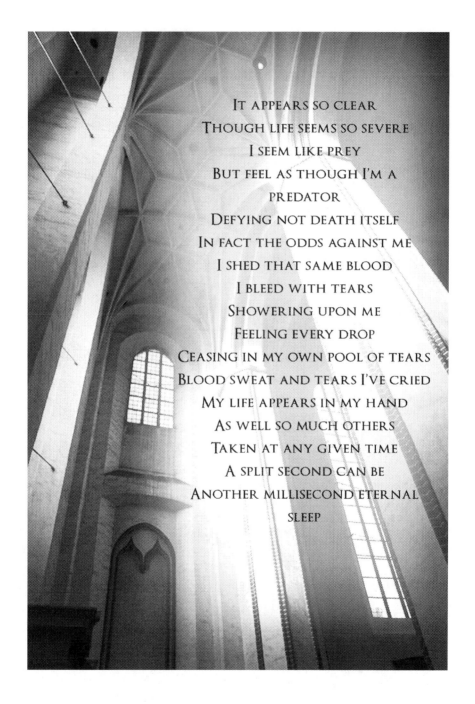

IT APPEARS SO CLEAR
THOUGH LIFE SEEMS SO SEVERE
I SEEM LIKE PREY
BUT FEEL AS THOUGH I'M A
PREDATOR
DEFYING NOT DEATH ITSELF
IN FACT THE ODDS AGAINST ME
I SHED THAT SAME BLOOD
I BLEED WITH TEARS
SHOWERING UPON ME
FEELING EVERY DROP
CEASING IN MY OWN POOL OF TEARS
BLOOD SWEAT AND TEARS I'VE CRIED
MY LIFE APPEARS IN MY HAND
AS WELL SO MUCH OTHERS
TAKEN AT ANY GIVEN TIME
A SPLIT SECOND CAN BE
ANOTHER MILLISECOND ETERNAL
SLEEP

You see within my inner circle
Blood, sweat, and tears
So many years fought constant reminders
So many pictures painted upon my walls
Stained colours traceable
Leading back to what once was
Seeing the past
Not letting a single day pass by
Look at life
Not through with it

Pictures have not passed
Nor have all the memories
Nothing seems tainted
Love wanting forever more
The understanding so deep and precious
Voice so heart warming
Telephone rings with such a heartbeat
Life on the other side of things
Once one had
Love speaks this name

Take a walk with me
In my dream everything seems so perfect
Wonderful and kind, love seems
No fear no regret seem evident
Above water we are
No gasping for air
Alive we are more than ever before

Take a look at my life
Filled with your presence
The essence of your beauty
The unremarkable scent of you
And your sunshine you deliver when never could be done

Take a look at me
I'm so frustrated
Hurting within me
I need that light once again
Take me your way once again
Your love seems destined again
Our souls seem destined again

Heard your voice
I wish, could
You fulfill my ever-burning desire
My complete dress attire
My soul feels on fire
Such the spark of your voice
Ignites a flame within
Stem so deep but able to make contact
Ablaze, creating heat
I crawl to knees in defeat

Visions of once being there
Cloud nine where you were mine
Child in love
Something I discovered in someone so beautiful
Love once knew me
Keeping my world intact
My heart a complete match
My heart open filled with so much abundance
Burning deep for your every existence
Everything about you
What made you, you
What made us a perfect match?
What made us detach
Two hearts not spoken
Left so much to say
Words so meaningful

Girl next door
Just a walk away
Love in my life
Love of my life
Love so spiritually deep
Heart so pure
A soul to cherish

Girl next door
Not a bridge too far to cross
So true to life
So many views to life
Such a mind to life
Such so many thoughts
Such an action

Girl next door
Closer than a phone call away
To my dismay
So full of life
So full of love
Love is life
Love is my every existence

I'm neither dead nor gone
I am the witness of my every shadow
My every movement is a calculated step
I bear witness to my past
Not knowing what lies in store
What awaits me?
Yet to be determined

I know not my complete sense of self
But my every thought and things
My corruption, frustration, what affects me
I know not my full mind capacity
But an idea of mind process

I stand witness to my every dream
For I was there
In my world where it took place
In the caves, fields, red, yellow, and black roses
Witnessing death
I died, but reality awakes my soul from dreams
I stand before you, neither dead nor gone

I am everything but different
I am what I am
What you see
The object as it appears before your very eyes
A nigger black, bold, and beautiful
So much to say so it does not appear
Take some time out
Listen

One life to live
Letting not a day pass by
So many days dark and confused
Mentally and spiritually dead at times
More days have transgressed this rhyme

This is the life
High as ever, no hydro
So much to never ignore
Intoxicated by the struggle
So many trying times
As days go by, they progress this rhyme

One life to live
This is the life
So much to claim
Living up to the name
As that pulse beats by

You cannot fathom to figure it out
The just of it
A piece of the pie
An inkling of it
Why it happens?
What takes place visually?

That soul emerging to the sky
Why it is the way it is
Why life can glitter at a particular moment
The next just seem like forever rain
Filled with dying pain
Plenty of suffocation
A yearn for oxygen
The just of a single breath
To survive that need

Death comes
Splurging that explosion of importance
Too late the coffin has arrived
Too little too late
That undying love has awoken
Eating within the depths of your core
Ever so alive
That it is, life as it is known

The talk of the streets
Leaving many to weep
In their pity and shame
I relish off this abundance of success
They think I am repressed even oppressed
Say what you say
Claiming whatever it is you dare
I've shed so many tears
So wide-open, a public
This is but a public appeal
I am everything but steel

I've born witness to those dark nights
Cold days
I've been through the storm
Never dearly departed
They say home is where the heart is
I am everywhere but home
In hopes one day I will be there
One day

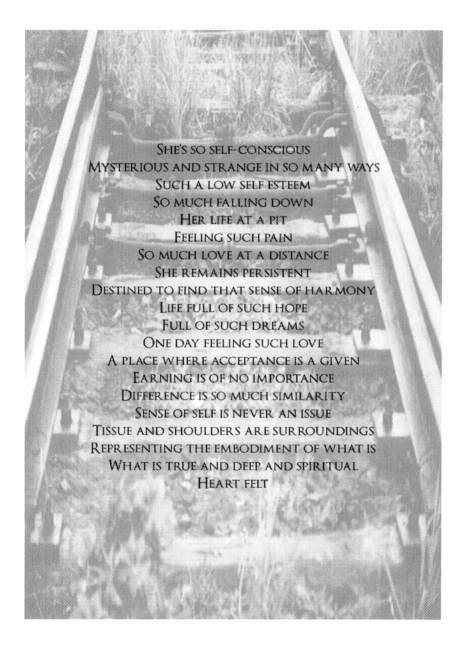

SHE'S SO SELF-CONSCIOUS
MYSTERIOUS AND STRANGE IN SO MANY WAYS
SUCH A LOW SELF ESTEEM
SO MUCH FALLING DOWN
HER LIFE AT A PIT
FEELING SUCH PAIN
SO MUCH LOVE AT A DISTANCE
SHE REMAINS PERSISTENT
DESTINED TO FIND THAT SENSE OF HARMONY
LIFE FULL OF SUCH HOPE
FULL OF SUCH DREAMS
ONE DAY FEELING SUCH LOVE
A PLACE WHERE ACCEPTANCE IS A GIVEN
EARNING IS OF NO IMPORTANCE
DIFFERENCE IS SO MUCH SIMILARITY
SENSE OF SELF IS NEVER AN ISSUE
TISSUE AND SHOULDERS ARE SURROUNDINGS
REPRESENTING THE EMBODIMENT OF WHAT IS
WHAT IS TRUE AND DEEP AND SPIRITUAL
HEART FELT

I am what the streets claim me to be
Everything and anything they could possibly claim
I've persevered; I've failed in front of the eye
My heart has died
I've been shocked back to life
I've been down on bended knee
I've been in the case of particular pleas

I feel that undying pain
Never showing that fear
For I fear not death itself
For death will come upon me
Till my dying day
Ceasing never to exist
I will stand tall

10 toes as well 10 fingers
I am human no alien
Just different in so many ways
Too many to describe
Despite my capability it has not been seen
They've looked within my eyes
Shedding was their perspective of me
Everything they could possibly see
Nothing ever displayed
Though it did
Blinded it was
For I was everything that they saw
Everything they made me to be

I am claiming no set
Earning my respect the old fashion way
A fusion of just being me
Not my choice of self
Claiming no line or face
Living me and nothing though me

Being me from the days of cradle
Till my days of unburied grave
Looking to the sky
For it holds everything that it prosperous for me
In me
My dreams fly for me; ride
Amongst the clouds
For there is my purpose
Claiming me and no set
A fusion for just being me

There is so much injustice
Failing to define this justice of injustice
For justice has not been served with any explanation
Explaining justice has not been reiterated
Taken into consideration for that matter
For there is so much injustice
Not enough justice to explain the injustice

The ghetto seems to have a mental telepathy; that no one seems to escape. For they have been blinded by that particular image of life; that they see for it all everything within this life is them. For they know not nothing, but this and or what they have been exposed to. So much imagery, dreams and the nightmares that have them secluded; eating their lives as we see away. They walk with everything but purpose and particular goal, surviving each and every day seems to be their means of living. Feeding that empty stomach, feeding off whatever knowledge that blows within the wind that happens to surpass them by. Lost souls seem to fly, but not the dreams for that odd reason, maybe oppression for that system seems to be putting bars before them limiting success providing that sense of boundary. In that brings on the years of coming depression for people are not equal, but different, and that's what separates them. They see not what they see, but what others envision and that follows painting pictures of what they see; forbidding looking within themselves to find that meaning to life.

Stand still. Listen to this game we play of hard knocks, shots beat this block, hitting a few who live by that lead taking that step forward they die by lead. Continuing to force the hand, risking losing their closest man. The circle refuses to live by the almighty bible; this life is all that is known. Behind bars, lying with a confession on their head plate; refusing to snitch, but to let their brother enjoy his freedom while they await destiny that lies in the hands of the lord. It seems that circle has a mental telepathy, new breed regains the position of old breed continuing with no sense of change. Corrupted by what they see, and not by the many dreams that float, committing life to nothing as it seems but is everything to them, what sense is there to visualize?

Contemplated decisions
Confused thoughts
Love in the air
Such a fear
Such a scare
My love is so sincere

I see deep within you
Deep within your core
A love for me so precious
So divine
Pure, deep, sweet

I've awaken within you
Awakened that sensitive side
Untouched love
Your care for me so steep
Your heart racing
Pounding, drumming, plummeting
So weak

My kiss, my touch
So true it is
My words false
Not true
These words I spew
Straight to your soul
To touch, hold, keep
I have everything it is you seek

Money, power, respect
Destination heaven
The power of the dollar
Holds so much cruelty and wickedness
Blood, sweat, and tears
Leak away as it passed through
Death and poverty
Hunger and malnutrition
Dreadful frustration
Leaving so many words to mumble,
But to whom?
Is that it?
So called development
So it is or perceived to be
So we shall
Or have we?
The time seems to have passed?
Embark with on any doorstep
Development they say
The roles they portray
People mislead
Development promoted but not fed
The people must die
The people must die
So they say

I've been withholding my anger
Refraining from committing to that stranger
That someone who seems to exist deep within
He pushes and he pulls for existence
Hounding boisterously
No backing down without a fight

Representing the flip side of things
Playing the opposite wing
On his guard ready to strike at will
To kill if necessary
Standing for everything that is not
Nothing that is meant to be

As time passed
Nearing closer and closer to his demise
He remains closer in disguise
The flame slowly dies
Perishing ever so slowly
Till it is a flame no more

I HAD A PURPOSE IN MIND
MY WORDS MEANT MORE TO ME
VICTORY SEEM SO SWEET
I AWOKE TO NOT A DREAM
A SENSE OF HOPE HAS ARISEN
THE CONSCIOUS REPEATED ITS PACE
WONDERING ABOUT TOMORROW'S FATE
"PIECES TO A DREAM"
ARISEN FROM "FAR FROM HOME"
WORDS FOR GREATNESS
YOU UPLIFT MY SPIRIT EVEN MORE
SEEDS OF DISPLEASURE DIED
I CAN PROSPER
THE DEPTHS OF CONCRETE
BETWEEN THE CRACKS GREW A FLOWER
PONDERING ARE THE THOUGHTS OF ROSA
MARCHING IS THE WISDOM OF MARTIN
OBAMA THE CHILDREN MUST FLY
SOAR MUST THE MINDS
ARISE MUST THE SOULS
THE PRISONS NEED AIR
THE WORLD NEEDS HOPE
TOMORROW IS MY PURPOSE
OBAMA WALK WITH ME
TAKE A WALK WITH ME
FOR IT IS I WHO STRUGGLE WITH FEAR
IN HOPES OF TOMORROW'S DESTINY
I AM TOMORROW'S EVERY HOPE AND DREAM OF
SURVIVING
THANK YOU

I'm living my dream, who ever thought I would be in this position to share this with so many souls. I'm out here with a muscle but my hands not tied behind my back. They may have my tongue tied, but they cannot stop me from writing this peace of mind and this freedom of mine. So on that let me speak this moment of clarity, and share with you all. I'm building this mind, muscle, through this struggle that I aim to conquer without any missile to lead me to this zone. Relying upon myself, and myself alone. Others have failed in proving they can co-exist with me along my journey to stardom by committing to so many actions. The actions they proclaim I want no part of that is why I want no one to take a walk with me. I journey to the unknown to such a land, dream, and memory whatever it is I aim to find it. I know not what I'm looking for when I find it I will know.

I am, I am
I am whatever it is I am
I am whatever it is I want to be
I am whatever it is you see
I am your wildest imagination
I am your selfless dream
I am whatever it is you see deep within your core
I am everything and a score for sure

Angel believes that she envisions what appears before her very eyes -me. She envisions I live this life above water, fighting for every breath of oxygen that I can bear to stomach from my lungs. I am in this fight against myself; where this battle between mind and self seem to collide in altercation. I was a man before I became a child, forced to pick up his scooter, run before walk, speak before spoken to, learn with no resource. Spell before I learn to read, teaching myself everything I could possibly imagine. I patted myself on the back when no one was there, when I stretched needing that sense of comfort and understanding, most importantly support. Angel sees so much in me, a result to her generalization of me, toward me.

They can't stop me from writing, can they? I've got too much in my heart right now. I apologize if anything becomes unclear from this point on; I'm staring in the mirror as I write this with an image of not me, but my mind, body, and soul. This seems like history in the making for me. I cannot speak but my fingers are mobile so let the jungle city kid speak because when I die that's what I was, still am, and forever will be. The kids run in the streets with pampers strapped at their side; mothers chasing, in hand a belt to fix that tail. It seemed like growing up in jungle city it had a mental telepathy. Some of the young bloods became dead bloods and it continued. The young gifted became nothing but a street statistic that had that promising future ahead of them but for one split second were able to trade it in for a gun and a badge to represent our city strip. However, I choose to represent it in a different manner. So many poetic verses I choose to spit of my memories; life in the fast lane, life in the dark, many wishes in which I had, the misery that I saw, all the abuse and so much more letting my strip know that I got this. It was labelled jungle city back in the early 80s, my home, home is where the heart is, and home is where my heart is.

I did not start this shit
But I will finish it if dared
I strike fear within your eyes
Believe me I can pop a surprise
I'm a blessing in disguise
It so simple to take your life
You have not a clue
Want to be gangster
Wake up and make up
You done fucked up now

So innocent, such a soul
Fighting within herself
Mind and heart trying to console
That you help unfold
Fuck this relationship we threw
You have no idea who I am
Business can become war
War leads to death
To your demise I can foresee
Everyone around you better fear me
The devil within me feels full control
All I need to do is point
You can get smoked like grown weed

What bothers me the most you still continue
I wish death upon no man
My blood sweat and tears are building
This anger and frustration I keep concealed within
It's boiling to begin
As we grow as men
We learn to let a lot go
But there is so much bullshit that I withstand
You can only step upon my toes so few times
I have no rep to withhold
Now I'm talking to you straight
Let's not let this situation escalate
Or a so-called soldier will be buried
The ground humbling your acceptance
I would love to see your resignation
Placed upon your life

A penny lies above your head
You're worth a bucket
I'm prepared to die for this
Ask yourself the same question
I got nothing to lose
Your death to gain

One night involved such intimacy
Oil dripping down your sweet skin
Through the crease of your spine
Flowing ever so smoothly
Down you're your back as it hits my palm

Stroking my hand up and down
Side to side
Across, back down, and up again
Nibbling upon your ear
Whispering such soft sweet words
Causing knots within
Conceiving you to give in
To my warmth and comfort
My lips ever so soft
Your lips brushing across
Breathing such energy of sympathy
Such a symphony
Such music flows
Soft brush kisses
Painted upon your lips

I want to see you smile
I want to be the reason you smile
I want you not in denial
You are my princess
Every inch of my core,
My heart and soul forever more

I want to see you smile
I want to be the reason you smile
I want to be every phone call you dial
You are my every thought
My every dream
Star I look at as dark beckons upon me
You're all that I see
You're the reason I smile
I want to be the reason you smile

I've been critically claimed everything that could be
Everything that the world foresees
I am everything that has been perpetuated
Undressed in the public eye
To some a blessing in disguise
Made a mockery deemed a coward
In that the public breathes such sour thoughts
In the past I've become a lost thought
I've fought and growled and scratched my way to the surface
Going back I've forbidden doing

I've been stained
My name spit upon
In that I've begun
To show signs of life and recovery
Fighting to live
Even though I'm living to die
Fighting to see
Though I see nothing inside
Fighting to give
But not blessed with the opportunity
I'm living to find
Whatever and whomever it is
In that I seek
I seek and I shall find

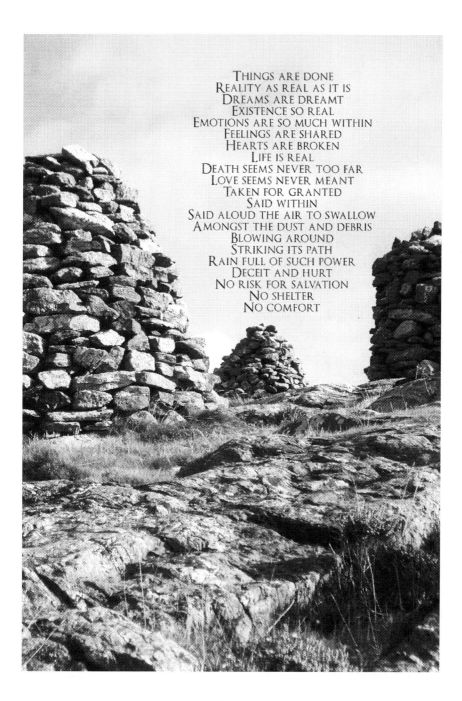

THINGS ARE DONE
REALITY AS REAL AS IT IS
DREAMS ARE DREAMT
EXISTENCE SO REAL
EMOTIONS ARE SO MUCH WITHIN
FEELINGS ARE SHARED
HEARTS ARE BROKEN
LIFE IS REAL
DEATH SEEMS NEVER TOO FAR
LOVE SEEMS NEVER MEANT
TAKEN FOR GRANTED
SAID WITHIN
SAID ALOUD THE AIR TO SWALLOW
AMONGST THE DUST AND DEBRIS
BLOWING AROUND
STRIKING ITS PATH
RAIN FULL OF SUCH POWER
DECEIT AND HURT
NO RISK FOR SALVATION
NO SHELTER
NO COMFORT

Pass me a pen
Get me a pad
Let me speak through this pen
Let me spit through this pen
If I can and if I may
Can I tell you the stories displaced?
If I can
Can I vent for a minute
In my moment of clarity
In that I expose all my sincerity
Sincerely to those who take a offence to the words written
To them I do not spit upon
But reveal my side
Hearing both sides
The object in the mirror is my reflection
Failing to see me holding within its grasp the physical form
Connecting with me not spiritually and mentally
Physically it can see me
But within me
It is and never will be me
It cannot envision me
But me
Make sense it doesn't
It fails to see the object of affection
The object attention
It holds me within the physical form

They paint the many pictures
The little fish in a big pond
They depict me to be
Figuring I'm through with it
I've got the mind of a hustler
Heart of a king
I've seen myself through the endless struggle
Hoping for brighter days
Failing to pay me my respect garnered
I continue to walk the streets
Searching for the unknown
Fighting to live
Dying to give
Misery seems to be my state of mind
I remain destined to find
A peace of mind
This heart of mine
Through hell, fire, and brimstone
Gladly risking it all

I gladly risk it all
Life or death the case
As it may be
My life on the line
In these trying times of pain and suffocation
No time to breathe
In this struggle to succeed
Not making a dime
Walking that thin red line
Through love and hate
Jealously and envy that so many embody
Looking at what I embody
The truth in me
The truth is I
There's no escape
I must see it

Live from the red stop signs and yellow lines
Where graffiti placates my mind
So many seem to find that state of mind
The struggle between conscious and decision
The fight in reality and dream
Depicting the difference among them

Where smoke crowds the air
Getting paid was the way raised
Living by any means necessary
Popping shot pellets relentless
Many times left penniless
Putting tracks to life
Displacing life off track

The hard struggle growing up in housing
Many walking heads low
No faith
Authority believing life was at odds
So many critically acclaimed frauds
I am a street calculus
I know my math
Cheating my way through life
So they perceived
So it is to be
I the streets
Like yellow lines on concrete
Stand before you
Making sense out of emotion

This is dedicated to the streets
The streets I am
The streets is within me
The streets raised me
Now I'm immune to it
It's all I got

I've walked the dog
I've been clouded in the found
The deep mist has crowded me
The streets have corrupted my mind
The media has painted a dark image
Poverty has lead me to believe
Africa finds it hard to survive
Sudan is concerned with funds
Building an economy is no solution
The people have no word
When they die so does hope
Life is left afloat
Swimming for survival
No concerns no worries
People left in a weary
This life seems so scary
I have no one near me
So many fail to see
I stand flooded in tears
Wondering when things are going to change
Hopefully in so many years

They've taken away my hunger
Left me with greed
Made me not a leader
Shedding no light on me
Forcing me to fight
Leaving me with no guided sight
To lead me, guide me
This is my life
My life alone

Made me a leader
Before I was ready to lead my own
I left many disowned
Things are not always as they seem
The past seems written
I continue to write everyday
Everyday seems a new chapter
Left for the soul to capture
I talk it like I live it
This is I
All I

My life: full of ink and paper that fills this very book containing my life, my very existence of who I am and what makes me. Life means alive and death seems eternal sleep. My life based on many values and beliefs; living to my dying day, providing a sense of hope to this dying breed who seem to be lost thoughts beaten out of their own minds and appear to be what they not know. I am what you not know but what you see. When I die I hope to have sparked a few minds and create bond by my words and peace of mind. I was always destined to represent and leave a stench never to be forgotten. This is my life!

The sky will fall
The sun will die
Not a day to survive
7 days will cease to exist
Pitch black
Not a moon to hover over
No light
Our hearts and soul to disappear
While darkness inherits the earth

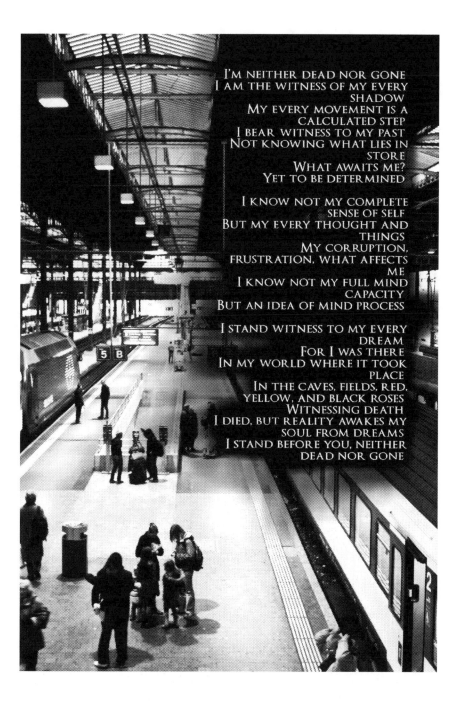

I'M NEITHER DEAD NOR GONE
I AM THE WITNESS OF MY EVERY
SHADOW
MY EVERY MOVEMENT IS A
CALCULATED STEP
I BEAR WITNESS TO MY PAST
NOT KNOWING WHAT LIES IN
STORE
WHAT AWAITS ME?
YET TO BE DETERMINED

I KNOW NOT MY COMPLETE
SENSE OF SELF
BUT MY EVERY THOUGHT AND
THINGS
MY CORRUPTION,
FRUSTRATION, WHAT AFFECTS
ME
I KNOW NOT MY FULL MIND
CAPACITY
BUT AN IDEA OF MIND PROCESS

I STAND WITNESS TO MY EVERY
DREAM
FOR I WAS THERE
IN MY WORLD WHERE IT TOOK
PLACE
IN THE CAVES, FIELDS, RED,
YELLOW, AND BLACK ROSES
WITNESSING DEATH
I DIED, BUT REALITY AWAKES MY
SOUL FROM DREAMS
I STAND BEFORE YOU, NEITHER
DEAD NOR GONE

Always content
To uplift another soul
Rise above all
Conquer my greatest fears
While following in the steps of my heart
Capturing my dreams
Wishing on a shooting star
Take advantage of par
Seize the moment

Infatuated with love
Everything about it
The many elements as many potions
As many mixes
The many procedures
As many corrections
Love
The experiment
Or so presumed to be

If I die
Don't you dare send me flowers
I rather a fire
In memory
Acknowledging my existence
Symbolizing my heart
Its brightness and passion to burn
Flames throughout the night
Till morning sunrise
Reminiscing me forever

My heart will never die
In each one of you
Lies my undying spirit
To be with you every step of the way
Till we are together again

I see you
What do you see?
Your mind a daze
You delusional
Multiple personalities
Which to decide next?

I see you
What do you see?
You look up
Clouded in darkness filled with emptiness
Where to go?

I see you
What do you see?
Crowding your head
Empty thoughts
Drowning in tears no apparent reason
What do you long for?

I haven't been blessed with this so-called gift. I have a deep passion to express this mind I have, let me tell you I find it quite intriguing. My life as an intellectual, though not accepted in this fashion. I always appreciated what was good for my mind

And didn't accept the many things I strongly disliked. A lot became of no importance to me; take it how you want to take it.

Love of my life
Lone star in the sky
Sun in my morning
My moon at night
Forever shining
Every hope
Every thought
Every wish
Every dream
My pillow at night
I hold ever so tight
A love so fine
Forever to be mine

Sometimes I forget who I am, my place in this world, and then come to the realization that this is my life because it keeps occurring. All this brings about is anger and frustration while I'm dreaming in this imaginative world I try to build in my mind. The perfect family, perfect relationship, and so on. I come to the realization that this world is imperfect and I had to accept that. Make no mistake, I value and cherish everything that I have, it's just sometimes it all feels short. I just have to learn to accept life as it comes.

My star shines bright at night
My moon sleeps so peacefully
My sun eats away at my skin
Leaving its hot remarks
Cold leaves me to quiver
Snow is as beautiful as it comes
Gently touching my soft skin
The cold I embrace
As it causes me to shiver with a steer
Knowing beauty is beautiful
Right before me
As I stare within

Black is darkness
Black I sleep to at night
Black is me
Black my eyes
Black my hair
Black my culture
Black for me
Black is me
Black is forever
Black I is I forever

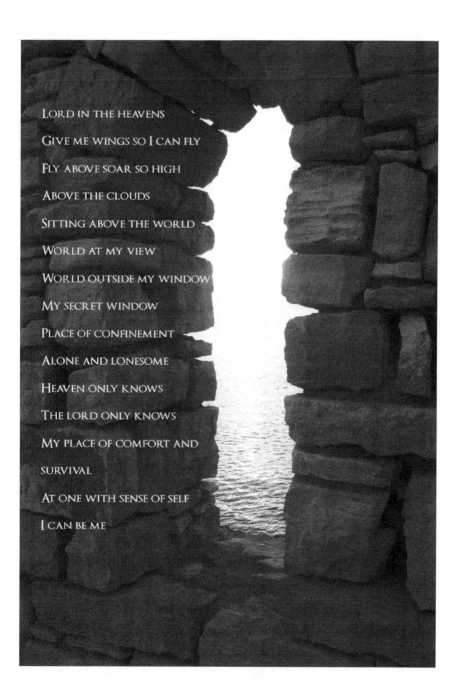

LORD IN THE HEAVENS

GIVE ME WINGS SO I CAN FLY

FLY ABOVE SOAR SO HIGH

ABOVE THE CLOUDS

SITTING ABOVE THE WORLD

WORLD AT MY VIEW

WORLD OUTSIDE MY WINDOW

MY SECRET WINDOW

PLACE OF CONFINEMENT

ALONE AND LONESOME

HEAVEN ONLY KNOWS

THE LORD ONLY KNOWS

MY PLACE OF COMFORT AND

SURVIVAL

AT ONE WITH SENSE OF SELF

I CAN BE ME

The day will rise that I cease to exist
Long before earth disappears
Long before god himself graces the world with his presence
Burn three candles
All of different colour
All different shape size and form
Different scent
Time span three days
Morning to night
Dusk till dawn knowing that I'm gone
Envision me in your mind
That divine human being
Self righteous and respectful
Privileged and successful
Honoured thy mother thy father
Bringing me into this crazed beautiful world

Now dying in peace
Heavens to uplift and unfold
Hell to bow beneath the lord
Take my soul so precious
My flesh left behind
Eaten away bits and bites
Till no more
I am free
Mind body and soul

Locked up 1 year
2 years
It seems like 5 to life
They caught you
Confiscated the shotty
Beating you senseless resisting arrest
So proclaimed

That is who you are
Never failing to express emotion
Never backing down
That was never an option in your vocabulary
That lion heart was born within
Symbolizing that courage, respect, honour and loyalty
To the red stop signs and yellow lines
That left many slain
Live and die for the streets
Blood sweat and tears
Never expressing fear

The ink is running out
I can no longer scream and shout
Never again to visit
My words sealed together
Take to heart
The penitentiary is no home
It is never to life
Home sweet home awaits you
Peace and one love

So many from afar, though darts my way
As if I were a target
Not mentioning my speech
This lisp that I project
So many words I have to say
So many words unheard
Not being heard was a solution not a suggestion
Can I be heard?
Can I live?
I considered a spade a spade
It is what it is
Not fake as real as it comes
As real as it is delivered
So real to life
Confused with conceited
I am what I depicted to be
Life in the flesh
The pain and agony I express
In that what a success
I feel not oppressed
I've left my nest
Breathing in this wonderful world of happiness

Set of two very few could match
Calibre and prestige
Such beauty and elegance
Voluptuous lips
Smooth faces
Light skin
Appearance so gentle
Long beautiful hair
Black shine
Such display of beauty
Curls of sensation
All shrivelled and bunched
Complicated in so many ways

Let me release you
Your inner soul
Who you are
What I seek
Every bit and inch
Every ounce

Afraid of love
Everything about it
Its touch
Its scent and fragrance
Its very existence
Be not afraid of me
Nor my love
Touch me
Hold me
Kiss me
Fear nothing

Let me die today
Forget that I ever existed
My life just a lost thought
Forget my very existence

I don't want the world to see me
I don't think that they would understand
Everything is made to be broken
My heart
My ties
My life
Let me die today
Forget my very existence
A lost thought
A distant memory
Let me drift away

I my own man
I make own decisions
I walk the path
Chosen lead by me
I walk the valley
So many men and women
What makes me different?

Indeed I am
So many ways leave me distinct
Ways in which indescribable
Indescribable to myself
As well to others
Others depict me to be different
Different in manner and style
Style of mind
Style of mine
Mind is mine
Mine I own
Me is me
You is you
They are they
We are we

Oppressed by the streets
Oppressed by authority
I'm oppressed by my mind
My heart and soul
Everything in me
To the bitter end
Life's a gift
A privilege so to say
You're here today
Not here tomorrow
Live from the cradle to the grave
Sun to the moon
To the stars at night
Risk yes
Fear no
Flowers bloom
People grow
In life you never know

LIFE APPEARS POINTLESS
DEATH SEEMS EVIDENT
IT'S EMINENT I'M GOING TO
DIE
LIFE SEEMS AS THOUGH A
GRAVE SHIFT
I CAN'T FATHOM LIFE
WITHOUT A STRUGGLE
LIFE WITHOUT THIS HUSTLE
MY PEN AND PAD
APPEARS THE ONLY THING I
HAVE
INKING THEN TO MY PRIME
YET TO HIT MY PRIME
IT'S JUST BEGUN
HAVING SO MUCH TO SAY
WHAT MORE CAN I SAY
SO MUCH ON MY MIND
SO MUCH TO MINE
THEY WILL FEEL ME
THIS IS GOD GIVEN
FREEDOM TO MIND
FREEDOM OF MINE

A life is born
A life taken
Nothing seems mistaken
Everything seems reason
People seek the greed and envy
The glory and prestige
I value existence
My life so to say
My friends love me
My enemies hate me
I am I
I can only be me

See me discreet
Discover me silent and motionless
Eyes pale
Body cold as ice
Feel the shiver
Perspiration at a high
A Negro dead
Body decay
Feel my heart thump
Open my eyes
All but a flashback
A figment of your imagination
Just a memory
I'm dead now

I am but a flower growing between the depths of concrete, mysterious but strange looking branch, ever so slowly. I am but a stem, a leaf that blows so swiftly. I am nothing short of spectacular; I am what I am but a flower growing between the depths of concrete.

Stand forward for it, I'm nothing special but a genuine man, a young man spreading his poetic justice, a love to write and rhyme. I write this love, expressing this creative mind, this poetic mind, similar to a love for music. I stay in tune with the belief of freedom for expression and a love for what I do.

Bless my mind
Bless my soul
My heart
Which endures all pain
My mind I express
My soul I exert
My heart I elevate
True faith I believe in
Death is a must

I seemed destined since birth
Destined to shine within my own spotlight
Even when they turned off the light
Locking me in the cage that became too deep
Leaving me frustrated and hurt inside
So many have tried
So many have died
Things are not always what they seem to be
In the darkness light has dawned upon me
Leading me not through the bars
But mind at ease and at rest
Resulting in salvation
They've controlled me physically
In attempts to leave me mentally impaired
Leaving me scared
They've given me a lot
Through so much struggle I have fought
In end I'm left with my pen and pad
The end

The darkness has escaped
Reaching salvation from its great depths
It was and still remains blind
Searching for light
Continuing with sense of hope

Feel my body thump from the grave
As you lay a body on mine
Alive he is alive he is not
What you thought was reality, it came to exist
Alive I am
A spirit amongst the world
My body left to decay
Left my heart and soul to persist
Living amongst the many hearts and dreams
I am that brush of wind
That every tingle when alone
That extra warmth at night
That body when needed
Dead, oh contraire
For my spirit still breathes today

Scream war
Promote peace
Four five shots
A poster
Relinquish the holds
Break the chains
Kick down the door
Smash the walls
Give up or succeed
Live or die
What do you believe?
One mind, one heart
I'm living and going
My soul here and there
My heart is everywhere

THEY CAN'T STOP ME FROM WRITING, CAN THEY? I'VE GOT TOO MUCH IN MY HEART RIGHT NOW. I APOLOGIZE IF ANYTHING BECOMES UNCLEAR FROM THIS POINT ON; I'M STARING IN THE MIRROR AS I WRITE THIS WITH AN IMAGE OF NOT ME. BUT MY MIND, BODY, AND SOUL. THIS SEEMS LIKE HISTORY IN THE MAKING FOR ME. I CANNOT SPEAK BUT MY FINGERS ARE MOBILE SO LET THE JUNGLE CITY KID SPEAK BECAUSE WHEN I DIE THAT'S WHAT I WAS, STILL AM, AND FOREVER WILL BE. THE KIDS RUN IN THE STREETS WITH THEIR PAMPERS STRAPPED AT THEIR SIDE; MOTHERS CHASING, IN HAND A BELT TO FIX THAT TAIL. IT SEEMED LIKE GROWING UP IN JUNGLE CITY IT HAD A MENTAL TELEPATHY. SOME OF THE YOUNG BLOODS BECAME DEAD BLOODS AND IT CONTINUED. THE YOUNG GIFTED BECAME NOTHING BUT A STREET STATISTIC THAT HAD THAT PROMISING FUTURE AHEAD OF THEM BUT FOR ONE SPLIT SECOND WERE ABLE TO TRADE IT IN FOR A GUN AND A BADGE TO REPRESENT OUR CITY STRIP. HOWEVER, I CHOOSE TO REPRESENT IT IN A DIFFERENT MANNER. SO MANY POETIC VERSES I CHOOSE TO SPIT OF MY MEMORIES; LIFE IN THE FAST LANE, LIFE IN THE DARK, MANY WISHES IN WHICH I HAD, THE MISERY THAT I SAW. ALL THE ABUSE AND SO MUCH MORE LETTING MY STRIP KNOW THAT I GOT THIS. IT WAS LABELLED JUNGLE CITY BACK IN THE EARLY 80S, MY HOME. HOME IS WHERE THE HEART IS, AND HOME IS WHERE MY HEART IS.

How do I begin?
Let me count the ways
Princess with the silver slipper
Awaiting true love at the alter
Hovered over her face white comfort
Causing a jaded vision
Lost and confused
Losing the true essence, now shallow
That special abundance of love
Once shared and felt so deep within her core
Those butterflies have taken departure
No longer flying without wings
Forced to build a cocoon once again
Never to fly again
Never to find true love again
True love once known
True love now gone

I look and see what is truly meant to be
A simple fatal attraction
I can fulfill your satisfaction
I want to be your simple reaction
I feel what I feel is real
This kiss has never been felt before
Feelings within feel so pure
So deep and rich are your lips
Soft and smooth
Caressing my lips forever more
You're everything I need and know

Coming too close to my heart
You've touched me in more ways than one
Undoubtedly I love you more and more
Two worlds clinging together
When we kiss the sky opens up
We are everything it needs to be at ease
In fulfilling its every need, want and dream
The sky dreams
It's been around never feeling this way
Feelings never to decay or wish to parish
Something heartfelt
Something so deep and cherished

The book is like the mind
Similar to culture
So to speak
Make you weak
Sad and cry
Never such a lie
Spit a poetic verse
Meant to curse
Evil, good, and bad
So many implications
Satisfaction and dissatisfaction
Promotions and great deeds
Love and art
Inspiration and salvation and comfort
Respect of self
Perspectives and views
Eyes meant to see
Ears as well to hear

Visualization of self
Meet or crumble
Books speak
Words speak
Food for thought
Sometimes shallow, cold, and resentful
Books are people
People are books
One is mind
The other judge for yourself

Who are you?
Who am I?
Who are you to spy?
My life's no mystery
Seems so hidden
A dark secret
Cast away
MY life's open to views
Ridicule my success
Ridicule my failure
Unhand me, forget me
It isn't possible to see
So I say
Who are you?
Who am I?
Open your mind

The world is one
A nation
A country
This planet earth
That can't correspond
Poverty it is
A dollar the case
The streets is war
People hate and deceive
This lifeless world
Motioning for peace
Breathes of love
Life's a gift
Cherish it

Let me die today
Forget tomorrow
6 feet
Ground humbling my acceptance
For I am just another body
Yet a different soul
Lifeless heart
Living soul
Live for the day
Seize the moment
Capture the memories
Wish on a shooting star
Today I lived
Loved and succeeded
For tomorrow is faith
My destiny
Another life to lead
I've lived by no bible
Nor religion
By none reason makes me no different
Simply creative mind
My heart and soul
Depicted decisions

This is an image
This is not an image
So many thoughts running through my mind
So many thoughts undefined
So many thoughts seem confined
So many thoughts defined
So many thoughts concealed
So many thoughts covered
So many thoughts ready to be exposed
So many thoughts of inspiration
Spoken in every word
So many words
So many thoughts
What's the meaning?

Lord in the heavens
Give me wings so I can fly
Fly above soar so high
Above the clouds
Sitting above the world
World at my view
World outside my window
My secret window
Place of confinement
Alone and lonesome
Heaven only knows
The lord only knows
My place of comfort and survival
At one with sense of self
I can be me

She's so self-conscious
Mysterious and strange in so many ways
Such a low self esteem
So much falling down
Her life at a pit
Feeling such pain
So much love at a distance
She remains persistent
Destined to find that sense of harmony
Life full of such hope
Full of such dreams
One day feeling such love
A place where acceptance is a given
Earning is of no importance
Difference is so much similarity
Sense of self is never an issue
Tissue and shoulders are surroundings
Representing the embodiment of what is
What is true and deep and spiritual
Heart felt

LET MY SOUL NEVER BE
DISTORTED
ALWAYS REMEMBERED
NEVER SPOKE DOWN
UPON
SPIT TO A DISGRACE
NEVER LOST IN SPACE
FOR I WILL BE
REMEMBERED
FOR ALL THAT IS GOOD
AND PROSPEROUS
ALL THAT IS LONGEVITY
FOREVER LIVING IN THE
HEARTS AND MEMORIES

So much more to life
So much pain in this game
This game is such a struggle
So hard to eat
Life seems such confinement
Bars holding me back
Within a place of discomfort
So much weary at hand
Only the heaven knows
This life of mine
This life of mind
The life I seem destined
The so many times I seem confined
Each and every my life seems on the line

At the tender age of six I was down
My mind and body and heart and soul down
I was down
I've been down
Knowing the individual within
Just another individual
Born but not raised
A part of the math
A statistic in this system
I was true
True to me
True to this is not an image
This is I
Never letting me down
True to my sense of self
Never losing to me

Take a walk with me
In my moment of clarity
Hear what I'm about
I shed these tears
Why I shed these tears
So many fears
What I'm all about
Why I scream and shout
Let this world feel me
Deep down they can't see
So many scars and scabs

Since the first night in it
I swore I would keep it real
Hated by many confronted by so many
Loved by very few

This is my life
Everything in it
Whatever which way they go
I turn the opposite
Committed to wrong direction
Turned the right way

A love forever
So to say
A dreamt dream
A shooting star
So to speak
A wish
You say
Life's beautiful
So I say
Feeling unexplained
Your heart forbids deep emotion
Do as the soul says
Soul's purpose
Goal in mind
A love forever
So I speak

Things are done
Reality as real as it is
Dreams are dreamt
Existence so real
Emotions are so much within
Feelings are shared
Hearts are broken
Life is real
Death seems never too far
Love seems never meant
Taken for granted
Said within
Said aloud the air to swallow
Amongst the dust and debris
Blowing around
Striking its path
Rain full of such power
Deceit and hurt
No risk for salvation
No shelter
No comfort

Soul searching
So destined to find
This true life of mine
Everything that fills my heart and soul within
The love once known
True love once a gift
Love so much cherished
Love so much yearned for
Love once to die for

Deeper than the ocean itself
Beyond heights of the very sky
Seen through the cloudiest sky
Every inch of me
My blood sweat and tears
I pour out every inch of my soul
To hear your very voice
Such warmth to my core

End all rumours and speculations
I did it and I confess to every bit it is
I confess to the serenity of love
Deep within me it seems a constant urge
This feeling seems indescribable
Dreams and fantasy occur rapidly
Constant repeated reminders
Thoughts racing
Feelings of such urge chasing
Fast enough for my imagination to capture
Soul left not to capture
Without further ado
I love you

I'm from the streets
The streets raised me
I've become immune to it
Never been baptized
Believed to have caught a spirit at least three or four times
People continue that same rhyme
Every day and every week

This is I
The image you see
God given mixed with so much
Dirt on my hands
Not an angel heaven sent
A being like so many that walk
Just another individual

An inspiration I am
An instrument with a voice
Here for a reason
Exploring my soul in this globe
In search of that vibration
An abundance of dedication
A rose in concrete
A card in a full house
One being
One voice
One mind
Let me be heard

Walk with me
Take some time and walk with me
Take a tour with me
Take a walk into my past
Take a look at the present

Many feel the presence
Feel the fear
Feel my heart beat
The tears sweat inside
I hide so much

Walk with me
Take some time and walk with me
Take a tour with me
Take a walk into my past
Take a look at the present

Can you see what I see?
Feel everything I feel in this world?
Is everyone a snake?
Or is there some motive to everything?
Is everything for purpose?

Walk with me
Take some time and walk with me
Take a tour with me
Take a walk into my past
Take a look at the present

Take a walk into this voyage of mine
Realize why I think everyone isn't so kind
Realize why people are so hateful
So ungrateful
What's in everyone's best interest
Is what I manifest
I live for

Walk with me
Take some time and walk with me
Take a tour with me
Take a walk into my past
Take a look at the present

What is this so called life?
What is loyalty?
I don't recall ever noting the definition
I don't know what's real anymore

Walk with me
Take some time and walk with me
Take a tour with me
Take a tour with me
Take a walk into my past
Take a look at the present
Was that so hard?

I stepped on your porch
I stepped on your paws
Fist fighting we continued
I love you to this day
Through hell and fire
We still remain thick through trying times
We walked the red stop lines and yellow lines
So many goals in mind
So much on our mind
So much to attain
So much remained unsettled
He left a void
Footprints all over
We spoke his name in vain
Left so much to gain
His loss
White powder seemed so important
White over black
The feigns made him
We made each other

After my departure
Let me rest and be weary
Do not shed a tear
For I am not out in the cold
Nor am I left astray
I stand beside our lord saviour Jesus Christ
I am with his son
Far not from you
So close within your heart
My soul rests
My spirit forever lives on
Let me die at peace to mind

Let my soul never be distorted
Always remembered
Never spoke down upon
Spit to a disgrace
Never lost in space
For I will be remembered
For all that is good and prosperous
All that is longevity
Forever living in the hearts and memories

Liberty has no name
Refrain from identity
Liberty speaks as does her soft lips
Such a soft spoken voice
Love speaks as well her heart
Soul speaks as if crashing waves
Her heartbeat sends shivers
Mental thoughts make my soul quiver
Such dreams seem never impossible
I can fly
I can fly

The bridge
The, the, the bridge
I claim lay to
My resting spot
I've earned my respect at home
The red stop signs and yellow lights
I walked through night and day
Pen and pad in my hand
Where I've scoped this gracious land
Land of hopes and dreams
Destined to capture
Wherever, whoever I lay eyes upon
My eyes on the prize
So much seems disguised
I can't hide forever
I must get out
I must come up

It appears so clear
Though life seems so severe
I seem like prey
But feel as though I'm a predator
Defying not death itself
In fact the odds against me
I shed that same blood
I bleed with tears
Showering upon me
Feeling every drop
Ceasing in my own pool of tears
Blood sweat and tears I've cried
My life appears in my hand
As well so much others
Taken at any given time
A split second can be
Another millisecond eternal sleep

Let me justify myself
What more can I say
In my moment of clarity
I know what girls like
Where I'm from
My first song
The upbringing
I've had a million and one questions
The city is mine
Friend or foe if so if not
You'll always be my sunshine
Threats and 99 problems
I've changed my clothes
Brushing my dirt off my broad shoulders
While the streets were watching
I've just begun to rhyme
You must love me

I have so much on my plate
I breathe the hunger for no more
I've met my appetite
Quenched my deepest thirst
My heart beats so fast
My soul rumbles amongst my mind
Making no sense it appears
Not knowing what's next
Feeling the deepest of dreams haunt me
Solidifying its dominance
It appears to take control of reality
I have not the courage to walk
Not the mind to seek
It is it could be
Reality seems imagination
Life seems a distant dream
Life seems a mile away

Life appears pointless
Death seems evident
It's eminent I'm going to die
Life seems as though a grave shift
I can't fathom life without a struggle
Life without this hustle
My pen and pad
Appears the only thing I have
Inking then to my prime
Yet to hit my prime
It's just begun
Having so much to say
What more can I say
So much on my mind
So much to mine
They will feel me
This is god given
Freedom to mind
Freedom of mine

Not known for blasting my chrome
Nor surpassing my own
Threats don't impress me
How dare you wish death upon me
I see the envy
You lust what I possess
You lust what I access
I've been oppressed
Straight from my umbilical cord
Through the wire
I walked I ran
I took my stand
I've been a savage
I've been afraid
I've been in that cage
I've walked on fire
I've drowned
I've blown the bubbles
Felt the cold air
I've shed tears of fear
I've vacated so much
I've been personified
I've been identified
Been condemned
Time to extend
Thanks and praise
Lord and saviour Jesus Christ

I feel like I can't vent into words
I struggle to fight
I struggle to breathe
My existence seems faded
Drifting away from the importance
True essence of life itself
True essence of mine
I love you too much to lose you
Your spiritual deepness
I know it may slip away
The way it use to be
The way it could be
The eyes in which I could see
Direction I was headed in
Detours along the way
People and destinations I wish to stay

Pictures are not for the wall
They remain a vivid thought
They remain not shaded
They remain not tainted
They remain not a memory
They remain a memory
Never making sense
But what you make of it
Life makes sense
Life makes not complete sense
Feel me
As matter a fact still feel me

I can't find what makes me strong
Rejuvenating my true heart
I once was he
I once loved her
I still love her so deep
My core deep within
The love to write
I cannot find again
I put my heart into it
I cannot any more
Maybe I am now

Maybe I did then
I know the reason no more
True purpose eludes me
Finding its way back
I don't know it's the hate frustration or hunger
Finding me to vent this
Life seems so pitiful
I find it hard to get through these stained tears
Feel me
Still feel me

I am the leader
The general of the opportunist
He who fears death, in denial
By your side
Along the way
To lead you not astray
Two thumbs
Eight fingers
Somewhere they're to linger with
Show you the hope and praise
The answers are plenty
By your side
By my side
Together as one

Darkness placates the city full of such bright light
Red stop signs and yellow lines
Love fills the air
Such places to go
Such a person to seek
Behind some door
Hidden amongst the shadows
Open such a mind not oblivious to love
Such a pain cannot be felt
Tears that bleed
Flooding the very streets
You cannot feel this love amongst the clouds
Deeper than the very sky itself
Pain no more
Love seeks such a shallow to find
In the mist of this very life

The truth and true ties
To that I testify
To every word written
To every word I spewed
It is I
It is I
I was gone and lost her
Explaining who I was
How I lost me
The critics rave
Deep down they love me
Offence taken
I had no remorse
Though some hatred with a need to vent
I aired it out
I swore to be real
In that I revealed
No periods airing it out
Opening it up by flipping the script
I was I
I am I was again
Not jaded with a need to break barriers
This could be my first and last log fire
I love you
If you love me
I hope to inspire
Refraining from holding back
Having so much to say
This love of mine that elaborates so fluently
Spitting this lisp of conscious
Words of wisdom for their wealth
Stressing the message to the unknown
The message unknown
For what it's worth
Take it
I made my choices
Feel me
Still feel me

Across the island
Separated by a beautiful body of water
She lies on the beach
My love and life
My earth, moon, and stars
Unforgettable, such a soul
Such a beauty
Waves crash, as does her mind
I'm on her mind
I am her mind as well is mine
She is mind and mine
I sit adjacent to her
Grasping the sand
Steering steep into her
Wondering dreaming
Mind at a daze
Nothing in particular
Love is this beautiful
Life is this beautiful
I've awakened this is not a dream
Reality as it may
Is mind and mine
I love you